ALEXANDER SOLLA

FINANCIAL MATHEMATICS
A STUDY GUIDE FOR EXAM FM

with 150 exercises

Poisson Labs

PREFACE

The purpose of this book is to help you pass the Society of Actuaries' exam on Financial Mathematics. The book covers all of the material on the official syllabus, as of December 2014. Just as importantly, it covers the material in enough depth that you can actually use the book as a primary text. Most importantly, it includes 150 challenging problems and solutions, and a practice exam comparable to the real thing.

In order to get the most out of the book, we suggest the following:

- Read a section and take notes, every day.

- Make flash cards, and review them every day.

- Do the problem sets a day or two after reading the relevant section. Try not to look at your notes unless you have to. The harder you try to remember, the faster you will learn.

- If you get a problem wrong, keep track of why. Was it a lapse of attention? Did you forget something important? Or was there a computational trick you hadn't learned? Make and review flash cards for the tricks and formulas you don't know.

- Keep track of which problems you find easy and which are hard.

- Once you have done all of the problem sets, do random selections of all of the problems you found hard, 20 - 35 at a time. Allocate 5 minutes for each problem. Work at a steady pace. Don't rush! We suggest doing this approximately once a week until all the hard problems are all done.

- Once you can get at least 90% on random selections of problems, take the practice exam, under timed conditions. Again, keep track of the wrong answers and dissect the solutions. If you can get a score better than 85% on the practice exam, you are doing great!

The aim is to collect enough information to let you focus your learning where you need it most. We can recommend Poisson Labs' *Prompt and Practical* flash card and practice exam systems to optimize learning. *Prompt* takes advantage of *spaced-repetition*, which automatically schedules flash cards so that easy flash cards are seen less and difficult flash cards are seen more often. The *Practical* practice exam system has hundreds of exam difficulty problems, and is tightly integrated with *Prompt*. *Prompt and Practical* will give you the confidence you need.

CONTENTS

Contents

1

PRELIMINARIES

1.1 ECONOMICS

1.1.1 *Markets*

Financial markets share a common vocabulary that may be unfamiliar to students of mathematics, and even students of economics. We will briefly discuss the structure of financial markets. From the perspective of an end-user, financial markets are formed in terms of a queue of buyers and a queue of sellers, ordered by the size of their bid. In other words, the buyers with the highest bids are at the front of the buying queue, and the sellers with the lowest *ask price* are at the front of the seller's queue. The *bid-ask spread* is the difference between the highest bid and the lowest ask price. Generally speaking, markets with a small bid-ask spread are closer to equilibrium than markets with larger bid-ask spreads. Intuitively, a smaller gap leaves less room for the equilibrium price to hide in.

If a new buyer enters the market, and wants to buy immediately, she must pay the ask price. Symmetrically, if a new seller enters the market, and wants to sell immediately, he must sell for the bid price. Alternatively, the new buyer or seller can merely place a bid, and wait (and hope) that the other side drives the price in their favor.

We say that a buyer is taking a *long* position, and that a seller is taking a *short* position. That said, these words are overloaded with meaning, and while the meanings are largely consistent, it takes familiarity with the topic to understand how they all fit together. For example, somebody who *needs* to buy an asset is said to be short that asset, because their pressing need effectively makes their position in the asset net negative. For example, consider the *short sale*. A short sale is a tactic where a trader borrows an asset, sells the borrowed asset, hopes for the price of the asset to decline, and eventually buys the asset back – hopefully for less than he sold it, but often times not – in order to return the borrowed asset. Even though he is a buyer, he is still short. His obligation to return the asset means he has a net negative position in the asset. The essential, if abstract and figurative, meaning of 'short' is *having a net negative position in*, whether this occurs from having sold it, needing it, or some other circumstance. Similar comments apply to a 'long' position.

1.1.2 *Risk and Risk Aversion*

Qualitatively describing risk is not straight-forward, particularly because the word has many different meanings. The essential notion is that a strategy is at risky if its outcome is uncertain. We can attempt to measure the risk using probabilistic measures, such as the variance or standard deviation of the outcome. A modern economist might suggest using the standard deviation of the utility of the possible outcomes. This measure certainly has conceptual appeal, but obviously, estimating subjective utility functions is not a simple matter. Using a proxy, such as monetary outcomes, has appeal and is practically useful, especially in cases where the person or firm measuring the risk has a *linear utility function*. The linearity of utility means that each additional dollar earned provides exactly the same utility as the previous dollar. More significantly, it means that this person or firm is *risk neutral*. We can differentiate between three categories: the risk averse, the risk neutral, and the risk seeking.

A person is *risk averse* if $E[u(X)] < u(E[X])$, where X is the outcome of a strategy. In words, if the expected utility of the outcomes is less than the utility of the expected outcome. Practically speaking, this means that a person weighs losses more than gains of the same magnitude. We can imagine this person playing a fair coin flip game for a dollar. The expected outcome is $X = \frac{1}{2}$. But if $E[u(X)] < u(E[X])$, then $\frac{1}{2}u(1) + \frac{1}{2}u(0) < u(\frac{1}{2})$. This person loses utility just by playing.

3

A person is *risk neutral* if $E[u(X)] = u(E[X])$, that is, if u is a linear function. A person or firm is *risk seeking* if $E[u(X)] > u(E[X])$. We can perform the same kind of analysis of the dice game with a risk-seeking person, and we would find that the risk seeker gains utility just by playing.

Risk aversion implies a willingess to pay in order to not have to take risks. In finance, paying to shield oneself from the consequences of a negative outcome is known as *hedging*. We can quantify how much a firm is willing to pay in terms of their utility function. In particular, let W be the firm's wealth, and let X be the result of a strategy. The firm is willing to spend up to the amount h that makes them indifferent between a certain loss of h and an uncertain loss of X, which we state formally as

$$u(E[W - X]) = u(W - h).$$

We end this discussion by distinguishing between two types of risk. *Systemic risk* is risk that exists throughout an economy. It is the risk that the economy as a whole will slow down or even effectively stop, for reasons such as inflation or deflation, *contagion* spreading from an important industry to the rest of the economy, the threat of war or terrorism, or even the misallocation of an important natural resource, such as oil. This risks are also called *non-diversifiable risks*, in contrast to the *diversifiable risks*. A diversifiable risk is an investor can *diversify away*. In other words, diversifiable risks are those that only specific businesses face. An investor can mitigate diversifiable risks to her portfolio by investing in a broad range of companies, in a broad range of industries and locations.

This brief discussion on diversification highlights one of the reasons people hedge. A typical firm's management team is heavily invested in the company, and it is unlikely that they have a diversified portfolio. Much of the value they have earned is at risk. This can cause their decision-making regarding the firm to be risk averse.

1.1.3 *Arbitrage*

Arbitrage-free pricing is a general method that allows us to set prices on financial instruments. *Arbitrage* occurs whenever different markets have set different prices on the same asset, at the same time. This means that a market participant can buy the asset for a lower price and immediately sell it on the other market for a higher price. Effectively, these are risk-free profits.

The *no-arbitrage principle* tells us that if the opportunity for arbitrage exists at all, it is unlikely to persist for long. We state the following argument here, once and for all, so that variations of it do not fill the body of the text: If somebody performed arbitrage, their buying would cause prices to increase in the less expensive market, and their selling would cause prices to decrease in the more expensive market. This would bring both markets to the same equilibrium price.

Arbitrage-free pricing is important in the theory of finance because it allows us to find the prices for entire classes of assets, all at once. For example, we will later see that we can construct a "synthetic stock" that acts just like the real stock it is supposed to mirror, by buying and selling other kinds of financial instruments. If constructing the synthetic stock cost more, or less, than the real thing, we could profit, at no risk, by buying one and selling the other.

Of course, we have been ignoring transaction costs in this discussion. We might be able to buy bananas in Costa Rica for less than in Chicago. That does not necessarily represent an arbitrage opportunity – although it might represent a business opportunity. The seller in Chicago has provided a valuable service that the seller in Costa Rica has not. The seller in Chicago has already imported the fruit. We can either pay the seller in Costa Rica for bananas and a shipping company for shipping, or pay the for bananas and let the American supplier handle transport. The no arbitrage principle tells us that if the market for bananas is competitive, the prices to get bananas in Chicago will be the same, no matter which method we choose.

In other words, the no arbitrage principle can tell us things that are plainly false, if we ignore transaction costs. It is very possible that the seller in Chicago has already entered into a long term shipping contract at rates we cannot get. We must take care when we use the no arbitrage principle. We must ask: is the market liquid enough for no-arbitrage to apply? Are transaction costs low enough for no-arbitrage to apply? Conversely, if we suspect we have found an arbitrage opportunity, we must ask: Are *my* transaction costs low enough that I can act as a market maker for this good at no risk?

1.2 PROBLEM SOLVING

1.2.1 *Rounding*

Effective use of rounding is absolutely vital to solving problems in financial mathematics. In short, the most effective rounding method is to never round at all. The next best method is to only round down when you are done finding the solution. This is the most realistic option.

We suggest using rounding as a sort of 'note taking' device. In the course of solving a problem, if you find a value for a variable, write down a rounded value for it. And write it down to 4 to 6 significant figures. Don't use it except for keeping track of which number in your calculator's memory to use. Using these rounded numbers will give a reasonable approximation to the solution, but it is error prone and time consuming to write a number down on paper and then to type it in to your calculator. This should be a last resort, not a common occurrence.

As a matter of fact, this is the method we use when writing problems and solutions for this book. Our numerical answers are there as guideposts to help you make sure you did your calculations correctly, not numbers you should *use* in calculations.

We have had good success with rounding to three digits after the decimal point, even in the course of problem solving. When doing so, we have seen our answers vary by up to 0.5 from the official answer. This is quite a lot, but we must reassure you: the exam is not trying to test your calculator or your rounding skills. The calculator's answers were always good enough to distinguish between the multiple choices to find the correct answer.

In short, use a sensible rounding method you feel comfortable with. Use it consistently.

1.2.2   *Technique*

When it comes time to take the exam, it is important to be able to do the majority of the problems quickly. And we mean *quickly*. Mastery of the material is important, but the exams are designed to test your ability to manage your time, as well. You want to get through the problems you know how to do over with as quickly as you can, so you can focus on the problems you have never seen before. To that end, we suggest that you

i. Write down what the question is asking you for.

ii. Write down an equation that makes use of the information you have, and involves the variable the question is asking for.

iii. Solve for the variable.

iv. Use your calculator to make numerical calculations, and draw an arrow from the relevant variable to the numerical answer, as discussed in section 1.2.1.

v. Put the numerical answers together, ideally using your calculator's memory.

It is important to have a problem solving routine. You will develop this routine with lots of practice. Practice solving problems the 'long' way, especially while you are learning. But when you review, be on the look out for 'short cuts'. Do you really need to write down that formula? Practice and experiment. Keep track of your scores, so you don't take 'short cuts' that hurt your problem solving ability.

2

THE TIME VALUE OF MONEY

2.1 MOTIVATION

People typically prefer to have access to money sooner rather than later. This preference is an empirical fact, but it is none-the-less theoretically important. This *time value* of money forms the foundation for the theory of interest. The time value of money is quantified by how much we *discount* income or consumption in the future, as compared to right now.

Let us consider a simple example. Suppose that you are offered a choice between $100 today, and $100 in a year. Which would you prefer? We must presume that you would prefer to receive this income today. You would have a greater range of choices regarding how – and *when* – you could spend the money, if you had it now. In particular, if you didn't want to spend it now, you could wait a whole year, and you would be exactly as well off as if you chose to receive the money a year from now. That is to say, the allocation where you receive the money today is at least as good as the allocation where you receive it in a year. If you take the money today, you have the option to spend it today, or tomorrow, or a year from now.

How much is this option worth? In an important respect, it is completely subjective. You must ask *yourself* how much you are *willing to pay* to have access to the money sooner rather than later. In other words, what is the least you would accept? Would you take $99 dollars today instead of $100 in a year? How about $90? $25? Your answer to these questions defines your *discount factor*, which we denote by v, and define as your answer as a fraction of the total you would receive in the future.

In an important respect, this question has a quasi-objective answer, as well. In particular, interest rates are set by people answering this question, in bond-market auctions. We will examine this situation more closely later, but for now, consider that interest rates are set by people bidding money today for income in the future. We will examine why this answer is 'quasi-objective' shortly.

This brief discussion on discounts does lead us to some natural questions. How does the discount factor relate to interest? Mathematically, the relationship is very straightforward. Recall that we defined v as the least you would accept for payment now, as a fraction of the amount you would receive if you waited for a year. Let us suppose the least you would accept is x, so $v = \frac{x}{x+y}$, where y is the amount you are willing to forego for income now. Then, we define the *interest* as the quantity y, and the *interest rate* as $\frac{y}{x+y}$.

Economically, we must examine the situation more closely. You are willing to forego some quantity to receive payment sooner. And there is a maximum quantity you are willing to forego. Let's call that y. If you are asked to forego more than y, you would choose to take the money in a year, because you would receive more utility from waiting for a year. If you are asked to forego less than y, you would choose to take the payment now. If we assume that your utility function is continuous, then y is the quantity that makes you *indifferent* between the two choices. You would get the same utility by taking the smaller payment today or the larger payment in a year.

And, in some economic sleight of hand, consider that foregoing payment for a year amounts to *giving a loan* for x today, and receiving x + y in a year.[1] So y is the amount that makes you indifferent between keeping your money and loaning it out for a year. y is your interest in the loan.

2.2   PRESENT AND FUTURE VALUES

As we noted previously, we *discount* income and spending in the future, compared to income and spending today. This

---

1 Suppose that this sequence of exchanges occurs: you take the amount x today. You immediately issue a loan for x, to receive x + y in a year. You receive x + y in a year. Ignoring issues like the risk of default, you get the same payoff whether you wait a year or issue a loan.

is an empirical fact, but it is the foundation for the mathematics of interest. The previous section offered motivation, but did not give us enough detail to actually solve problems. We begin that process now.

We have discussed cash flows informally, but we must make certain facts and notations explicit. We define a *cash flow* as a certain amount c_t of money changing hands at a particular time t. The amount of money that changes hands is denoted by c_t. A sequence of cash flows can be expressed as $\{c_t\}$ or as $\{(c, t)\}$ when we need to disentangle the the amount's 'dependence' on time.[2] We also denote the space of cash flows by $\{c_t\}$. We adopt the convention that sequence written as a sequence of numerals begins paying today, unless otherwise indicated. We can also draw *cash flow diagrams*, like this one for the sequence $\{-1, 1, 1, 1, 1, 1, 1\}$.

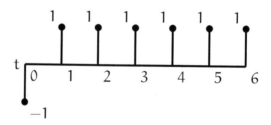

The stems above the axis represent income, and the stems below the axis represent expenditures. Unless otherwise stated, we assume the leftmost point on the axis represents

---

2 Consider again our example of getting 100 today or in a year. You will get 100 whether we call the amount c_0 or c_1. We sometimes want to vary the time without worrying about the name.

$t = 0$. This corresponds with our convention for numerical sequences.

We define a *period* to be the interval of time between successive cash flows. A period is the unit of time with which we perform discounting and accumulating operations. The length of a period is important, because we typically discount cash flows farther in the future more than cash flows closer to the present. A hundred dollars tomorrow is not much different than a hundred dollars today. We would not discount a hundred dollars tomorrow very much. We would discount a hundred dollars a year from now much more. As an empirical rule, the discount factor is a function of the length of the period we are discounting.

This example illustrates another principle. If we choose the length of our periods to be a day, a cash flow a year from now is 365 periods away from today. So how do we choose our periods? We must choose a unit that makes the calculations easy! In our motivating example, our period was one year. If you are calculating the present value of your rent or mortgage payments this year, you would probably want to use monthly periods. If you are dealing with bonds, you would typically use semi-annual (six month long) periods. We can even treat time as a continuous quantity and have 'periods' that consist of real numbers.

We define the *effective rate of discount* to be the amount, in percentage terms, that is discounted over a single period. We typically denote the effective rate of discount by d if it is constant, or by d_n for the effective rate of discount for the nth period. We also define the *effective rate of interest* to be the amount of interest earned in a single period. We typically denote the effective rate of interest by i, or i_n, for the effective rate of interest earned during the nth period.

We are now in a position to define the present value of a sequence of cash flows. Suppose that you are to receive $c_1, c_2, \ldots, c_n$ cash flows, and that the kth payment occurs at the end of the kth period. Suppose that we have a constant effective rate of discount. Then, the *present value* V of the sequence of payments is

$$V\{c_i\} = c_1 v^1 + c_2 v^2 + \cdots + c_n v^n. \tag{1}$$

Notice that we are discounting the first payment *once*, since we must wait a single period to receive it. And we are discounting the second period twice: we discount it for the first period that we must wait for the payment, and then again for the second period that we must wait. This should make intuitive sense. If we wait a period and receive the first cash flow, we still need to wait a another period to receive the second. In general, we discount the payment in the kth period k times.

We can also compute the present value of cash flows that already occurred. The simplest example is a single payment of 1 one period ago. In asking what its present value is now, we are asking an equivalent question: what was its value one period in the future, *then*? That is to say, the present value of a payment is the future value of the payment *in the past*. To that end, let us define a *fast-forward* function. Define the function $\kappa \colon \{c_t\} \to \{c_t\}$ by

$$\kappa\{(c, t)\} = \{(c, t - 1)\}.$$

Intuitively, κ lets us 'fast forward' time itself, so that every payment is due one period sooner. We can define the *fast-forward factor* κ by

$$\kappa = \frac{(\Phi \circ \kappa)\{c_i\}}{\Phi\{c_i\}}.$$

It is straight-forward to expand and simplify this expression, to find that $\kappa = v^{-1} = 1 + i$. Multiplying a cash flow amount by κ has the same effect on its present value as moving the cash flow one period back in time. And so, now we can see how to find the present value of cash flows in the past. We move each cash flow one period into the future, and multiply it by κ to undo the effect of discounting for an extra period.

The present moment is a moment in time like any other. We can compare the value of a cash flow now to one in the past, or in the future. By discounting or fast forwarding, we can even compare the value of cash flows at arbitrary periods. The present value is particularly convenient, however, because long term economic and financial planning requires us to make decisions about the future now.

2.3   ACCUMULATION FUNCTIONS

An accumulation function tells us the amount of money in an account has accumulated due to interest at any given time. We say that a function a is an *accumulation function* if

1. $a(0) = 1$,

2. $a'(t) \geq 0$.

We can also define the *amount function*. A function A is an amount function if it can be written in the form

$$A(t) = A \cdot a(t),$$

where A is some amount of money. Indeed, the accumulation function measures how much an investment of 1 earns due to interest, and an amount function measures how much an investment of A earns.

There are a few basic examples of accumulation and amount functions, each corresponding to a schedule for discounting and distributing interest. For example, we have *simple interest*, where, at a rate of interest i and for an investment of A, an amount Ai is added to the account at every period. The accumulation function, then, is

$$a(t) = 1 + it,$$

and the amount function is

$$A(t) = A + iA = A(1 + it)$$

We also have *compound interest*. In this payment scheme, previous interest payments earn interest in the current period. For example, at a rate i, the an investment of 1 earns i in the first period, so that the account accumulates $1 + i$ in the first period. In the next period, the investment earns $i(1 + i)$ – interest is applied to the entire amount in the account. This means that the total balance in the account, at the end of the second period, is $1 + i + i(1 + i) = 1 + 2i + i^2 = (1 + i)^2$. In general, the amount in the account at the end of the tth period is

$$a(t) = (1 + i)^t,$$

and the amount function is

$$A(t) = A(1 + i)^t.$$

We see that the amount accumulated at time t, by an account earning compound interest, is the original amount fast-forwarded t times. Compound interest is the most important of the interest rate schemes, because of this mathematical correspondence with the time value of money.

We can calculate the effective rate of interest for an account using either the accumulation or amount functions. We define I_n to be the interest earned between times n and $n + 1$. The effective rate of interest earned between time n and $n + 1$ is

$$i_n = \frac{a(n + 1) - a(n)}{a(n)} = \frac{A(n + 1) - A(n)}{A(n)} = \frac{I_n}{A(n)}.$$

For compound interest, i_n is always i, the rate at which the account compounds. For simple interest, the effective rate decreases over time, since

$$i_t = \frac{a(t + 1) - a(t)}{a(t)} = \frac{i}{a(t)}.$$

The larger the account becomes, the smaller the proportion of interest earned.

A mathematically inclined reader may notice that the effective interest rate formula for the accumulation function bears a similarity to the derivative $a'(t)$. This is valuable intuition, which guides us to the *force of interest*. The force of interest $\delta(t)$ is defined by

$$\delta(t) = \frac{a'(t)}{a(t)} = \frac{A'(t)}{A(t)}.$$

This is a differential equation, but the solution is straightforward. We can recover $a(t)$ from $\delta(t)$ as the quantity

$$a(t) = \exp\left[\int_0^t \delta(t)\,dt\right].$$

We can derive another useful formula. Since $\delta(t) = \frac{a'(t)}{a(t)}$, we can calculate the amout of interest earned between times a and b by

$$I_{(a,b)} = \int_a^b a(t)\delta(t)\,dt. \tag{2}$$

For continous compound interest, the force of interest is $\delta(t) = \log(1+i)$. Since the force of interest is constant, we simply call it δ. Indeed, continous compounding is the only interest rate scheme with a constant force of interest.

We have been treating the accumulation and account functions as describing what would happen to an amount deposited into an account, if the account is left alone until time t. This is true enough, but realistically, we must handle situations where deposits and withdrawals are made to the account. Although there is a conceptual difference between deposits and interest earned, mathematically, they both merely add to the account. The important point is that a deposit only earns interest *after* it has been placed in the account.

It can be useful to blur the distinction between deposits and interest. We shall see several examples in the exercises.

Before then, we will introduce a useful formula for dealing with accounts with continous deposits that earn interest continously. Suppose that an account has deposits made continously at the rate $d(t)$, and that the account earns a force of interest $\delta(t)$. Then, the accumulated value at time t is

$$\int_0^t \left(\exp \left[\int_x^t \delta(t)\, dt \right] \right) d(x)\, dx.$$

2.4 PRICES, PROFITS, AND VALUE

Consider a cash flow that pays 100 in a year. We have already discussed the present value, so we have a good idea how much we would pay to have access to it today. We would pay 100d in order to have 100v today instead of 100 in a year.

Now let us consider a slightly different situation. Suppose that we were offered 100 in a year. How much would you be willing to pay to *buy* a claim to the 100 in a year? We already have the answer to this question, since buying a cash flow of 100 in a year, by paying P today, is the same as loaning P and earning $\frac{100}{P} - 1$ interest. In other words, we see immediately that P = 100v. This is a general phenomenon.

The *basic pricing principle* tells us that the *price of an asset is the present value of the cash-flows it generates*. We can see this must be true using the no-arbitrage principle.

But we must distinguish between the price of an asset and its net present value. An asset's *net present value* is the present value of all its cash flows, including any cash flows required to purchase the asset. For example, if you loan out $P = 100\upsilon$ today and receive 100 in a year, the net present value will be 100v − P. Notice that we have two kinds of interest in play here. The v in the equation is related to *your* time value preferences, where as υ is the discount factor for the interest earned by the loan – which is presumably higher than your own interest rate preference.

The net present value is also a special case of what we call 'profit.' The *profit* for a asset at time t is the accumulated value at time t of all of the cash-flows generated by the transaction. This explicitly includes the costs of purchasing the asset.

Because of the basic pricing principle, we see that assets don't generate profits unless unexpected positive results occur – the expected results are already factored into the market price.[3]

---

3 Modern physics tells us that matter, energy, and information are all *the same*. We can certainly see the value of information – it is money. This is not merely a glib observation; thermodynamic models, such as the

2.5 MEASURING INTEREST

2.5.1 *Nominal Rates*

Because the length of a period and discount rate are inter-related, one can't truly report one without reporting the other. Financial professionals commonly use a convention to communicate interest rates. They use *nominal rates*. Suppose that i is the yearly effective rate of interest. The *nominal yearly rate of interest, convertible m times*, is the rate $i^{(m)}$ defined by

$$\left(1 + \frac{i^{(m)}}{m}\right)^m = 1 + i.$$

The purpose of this convention is two-fold. As we said, we want to be able to communicate the length of a period in addition to the interest rate, and the superscript m gives us an indication. Indeed, m is the number of periods into which we are dividing the year. For example, if we are talking about $i^{(12)}$, we are certainly talking about monthly interest rates.

The other reason that the convention exists in this form is that it makes $\frac{i^{(m)}}{m}$ the effective m-thly rate. For example, $\frac{i^{(12)}}{12}$ is the effective monthly rate.

Wiener process, have become commonplace in economic theory, as you will see in Exam MFE.

We can convert between $i^{(m)}$ and $i^{(n)}$ easily. We simply plug one into

$$\left(1 + \frac{i^{(m)}}{m}\right)^m = \left(1 + \frac{i^{(n)}}{n}\right)^n$$

and solve for the other. There is a direct formula for this conversion, but it is done so commonly it will surely become muscle memory.

We have a similar formula for nominal discount rate. Let d be the effective yearly discount rate. Then the *nominal yearly discount rate, convertible m times* is the quantity $d^{(m)}$ defined by the equation

$$\left(1 - \frac{d^{(m)}}{m}\right)^m = 1 - d$$

Again, we can convert between nominal discount rates for different frequencies:

$$\left(1 - \frac{d^{(m)}}{m}\right)^m = \left(1 - \frac{d^{(n)}}{n}\right)^n$$

Indeed, since the effective discount rate is related to the effective interest rate by

$$(1 - d)^{-1} = 1 + i,$$

we can convert between nominal discount rates and nominal interest rates, with

$$\left(1 - \frac{d^{(m)}}{m}\right)^{-m} = \left(1 + \frac{i^{(n)}}{n}\right)^n.$$

2.5.2 *Yield Rates*

The *yield rate* for an investment is the rate of interest for which the present value of all the contributions into the investment equals the present value of the returns. The yield rate is also called the *internal rate of return*, or IRR.

Formally, the internal rate of return for a sequence $\{c_t\}$ of cash flows is the interest rate i which satisfies

$$\sum c_t v^t = 0. \tag{3}$$

The yield rate is theoretically the 'best' measure of the performance of an investment. Unfortunately, it has several problems. In particular, there are common cases when the equation has multiple solutions for the discount factor v, and so has multiple yield rates. The other practical problem is that 3 is a polynomial equation. As we know, there is no general method to solve high degree polynomial equations. Iterative methods can be used to approximately solve high degree polynomials. Indeed, this is how electronic calculators and computers compute the yield rate.

However, the financial instruments we discuss in this book all have well-defined yield rates.

2.5.3 *Time Weighted Yield Rate*

Several methods have been developed to address the difficulties of using the internal rate of return. One of these is the time weighted yield rate, which we will discuss presently. The money weighted yield rate will be discussed shortly.

Consider an investment account. We would like to measure the yield obtained by putting money into the account. One difficulty is that we can realize gains by selling portions of the account and withdrawing funds. This difficulty can easily cause the internal rate of return to not be unique. So we define the time weighted yield rate. To that end, let c_k be the kth *contribution* or *withdrawal*. These are the cashflows that the owners of the account make, as opposed to cashflows generated by the investments themselves. Let b_k be the account balance just before the kth contribution occurred. That is, let b_k be the present value of the account holdings, including cash, at the time the kth contribution occurred. We define the rate j_k by

$$1 + j_k = \frac{b_k}{b_{k-1} + c_{k-1}}.$$

Then, we define the time weighted yield rate j by the equation

$$1 + j = (1 + j_1)(1 + j_2) \cdots (1 + j_n).$$

The intention is to attempt to construct a yield rate that acts like an effective interest rate, using the times at which the transactions occur to delimit the periods. Each j_k is the effective rate of gain or loss since the last period, which only reflects the performance of the holdings.

26

2.5.4 *Money Weighted Yield Rate*

The money weighted yield rate[4] is another method for calculating the yield of a portfolio with contributions. Let c_t denote a contribution or withdrawal at time t. Let A be the account balance at the beginning of the year, and let B be the balance at the end of the year. Define the total interest I by

$$I = B - A - \sum_t c_t,$$

and define the money weighted yield rate i by

$$i = \frac{I}{A + \sum_t (1 - t)c_t}.$$

Let us examine the denominator more closely. Notice that the contributions are weighted by the quantity $1 - t$. That means that, for the purposes of calculating a 'nominal amount' which earns interest, we only count the contributions for the fraction of the year in which they are in the account – in other words, from the moment funds are deposited or withdrawn until the end of the year. t is typically expressed in terms of months, and possibly fractions of months.

---

4 This is also known as the 'dollar weighted yield rate.'

2.5.5   *Portfolio Yields*

In a pooled investment fund, a professional fund manager manages a large pool of investments. These investments are financed by the manager's customers, who expect that the fund manager will enter into profitable investments, in line with the fund's charter and philosophy. But how are the earnings allocated to the customers?

In the *portfolio method*, each contributor receives a pro-rata share of the investment's earnings for the year. The earned yield is calculated for the entire portfolio, and each account is credited at the yield rate.

But consider a situation where there are rapidly rising interest rates. If the investment portfolio contains investments made before the rate change, the older investments could hurt the portfolio's yield. New investments made by the fund will earn at the prevailing rates, but the older investments could earn at the old rates. This would make pooled investment funds unattractive to investors, because they could easily earn at the higher rates by buying securities at the new rates.

The solution is to maintain several portfolios, each of which represents a year in which funds were added to the investment account. In this way, each investor earns the portfolio yield for the portfolio created the year she began investing. She will not be paying for a pro-rata share of older, under-performing investments, but only for a share of newer, better performing investments. This is called the *investment year method*. Note that the opposite occurs if interest rates decline – in particular, the investor would prefer pooled investment funds that use the portfolio yield method during periods of declining interest rates, since she would gain access to funds earned by better performing, older investments. The rate earned by new deposits is called the *new money rate*.

Deposits made to pooled investment funds using the investment year method are typically moved to a common account after a certain number of years – 5 to 10 years is fairly common. Essentially, this common account uses the portfolio yield method, and does not keep track of the year in which deposits were made. There is little benefit to maintaining the funds segregated by the year they were deposited, once interest rate volatility has settled down for a number of years.

There is some notation associated with these concepts. Let y be the year in which funds were deposited to a pooled investment fund. Let k be the number of years since y. Under the investment year method, the interest earned during the year $y + k$ is denoted by i_k^y.

The portfolio method rate earned during the year y is denoted by i^y. For comparison, the interest earned in the year $y + 1$, under the investment year method is i_1^y, while the interest earned using the portfolio year method is i^{y+1}.

A pooled investment fund typically reports the yields in a table similar to table 1.

Investment Year	i_1^y	i_2^y	i_3^y	i_4^y	i_5^y	i^{y+5}
2004	6.1	6.3	6.2	6.4	6.6	6.6
2005	6.2	6.3	6.3	6.5	6.3	6.8
2006	6.1	6.2	6.2	6.4	6.4	6.9
2007	8.7	8.8	8.7	8.6	8.9	7.3
2008	8.8	8.9	8.3	8.4	8.4	7.8
2009	8.7	8.9	9.1	8.7	8.6	8.3
2010	9.0	9.1	9.2	9.0	8.9	
2011	9.3	9.2	9.3	9.1		
2012	9.1	9.2	9.2			
2013	9.2	9.1				
2014	8.9					

Table 1: The yield rates, broken down by year, for a pooled investment fund. Notice that the portfolio rates trail behind changes in the investment year rates, since the portfolio rates weigh older investments more heavily than new ones.

2.6   EXERCISES

Time Value of Money

1° Suppose that $v = 0.91$. Compute the present value of the sequence of yearly payments $\{30, 0, 40, 0, 55\}$, starting in a year.

2° You have been promised a payment of 35 per month, starting at the end of the month, *forever*. How might we define the present value of such a cash flow? If $v = 0.88$, what is the present value?

3° Suppose that your discount factor is 0.85, and let

$$\{-100, 0, 0, 40, 50, 60, 70\}$$

be a sequence of cash flows starting today. If somebody offered you this sequence, would you accept? Explain.

4° An infinite sequence of payments starts today at 100 and decreases by 1.1% each period. It is found that the present value is 1521. What is v?

5° Show that $1 - d = v$, $i = \frac{1}{v} - 1$, and $d = iv$. Confirm that $\kappa = v^{-1} = 1 + i$.

6° Recently, the cash flow sequence $\{0, 100, 100\}$ sold for 188.61. What is the effective interest rate?

7° Let $v = 0.94$, and suppose the present value of the sequence of cash flows $\{0, c, c, c, c, c\}$ is 103. What is c?

Accumulation Functions

8° Calculate i if, under compound interest, $a(10) = 2.159$.

9° Let $i = 0.09$. Find n such that $a(n) = 1.412$, under the assumption of compound interest.

10° Prove that for compound interest, the effective rate of interest i_n equals the compounding rate of interest i

32

11° At the start of each year, Brenda deposited the following amounts into her savings account. At the time each deposit was made, the bank was offering the interest rate for the year.

Deposits	Interest
100	0.08
100	0.075
50	0.07
50	0.065

How much did she accumulate?

12° Account A earns simple interest at the rate $i = 6.5\%$. Account B earns compound interest at the same interest rate. At time $t = 0$, 100 was deposited into account A and 50 was deposited into account B. These accounts both earned the same amount of interest at time n. Find n.

13° An account earns interest with force

$$\delta(t) = \frac{0.0125 + 0.0125e^{0.0125t}}{0.0125t + e^{0.0125t}}.$$

What is the equivalent compound interest rate for the time between $t = 0$ and $t = 5$?

14° An account earns interest with force

$$\delta(t) = -\frac{0.05e^{-0.05t}}{2 - e^{-0.05t}}.$$

What is i_{10}?

Nominal Rates

15° Convert the yearly effective rate of interest $i = 12\%$ into a nominal rate convertible monthly.

16° Convert the yearly effective rate of interest $i = 8\%$ into a nominal rate convertible semiannually.

17° Convert $i^{(4)} = 9\%$ to $i^{(6)}$.

18° Convert $d^{(2)} = 5\%$ to $i^{(3)}$.

19° Convert $d^{(2)} = 9\%$ to $i^{(12)}$.

20° Suppose that

$$\left(1 + \frac{i^{(k)}}{k}\right)\left(1 + \frac{i^{(2)}}{2}\right) = \left(1 + \frac{i^{(6)}}{6}\right).$$

Solve for k.

21° Suppose that

$$\left(1 + \frac{i^{(k)}}{k}\right)\left(1 - \frac{d^{(2)}}{2}\right) = \left(1 + \frac{i^{(12)}}{12}\right).$$

Solve for k.

Yield Rates

22° Compute the yield rate for the sequence

$$\{-40, 0, 30, 0, 60\}.$$

23° Compute the yield rate for the sequence

$$\{-10, 1, 2, 3, 4, 5, 6, 7, 8, 9, 10\}.$$

35

Reporting Rates

24°

Date	Balance	Net Change
Jan. 1	1500	–
Feb. 1	1525	-25
Mar. 1	1530	-25
Sep. 1	1535	-25
Jan. 1	1550	–

The table lists an account's transactions for the year. The balance column lists the account balance before the change on that date. What is the time weighted yield for the account?

25°

Date	Balance	Net Change
Jan. 1	1200	–
Feb. 1	1100	X
Mar. 1	1100	X
Jan. 1	1200	–

The table lists an account's transactions for the year. The balance column lists the account balance before the change on that date. It is known that the time weighted yield j is 6.5%. What is X?

26° An account starts the year with a balance of 1200. Contributions of 50 are made at the beginning of March, June, September, and December. The account balance at the end of December is 1600. What is the dollar weighted yield rate?

27° An account starts the year with a balance of 1000. A withdrawal of 600 is made on April 15, and deposits of 300 are made at the beginning of October, November, and December. The money weighted yield rate for the year is 6.9%. What is the account balance at the end of the year?

28° Refer to table 2 to find the total accumulated value for a deposit of 100 made in 2008 and withdrawn at the end of 2011.

29° Refer to table 2 to find the total accumulated value for a deposits of 100 made in 2008, 2009, and 2010, and withdrawn at the end of 2011.

Investment Year	i_1^y	i_2^y	i_3^y	i_4^y	i_5^y	i^{y+5}
2004	6.1	6.3	6.2	6.4	6.6	6.6
2005	6.2	6.3	6.3	6.5	6.3	6.8
2006	6.1	6.2	6.2	6.4	6.4	6.9
2007	8.7	8.8	8.7	8.6	8.9	7.3
2008	8.8	8.9	8.3	8.4	8.4	7.8
2009	8.7	8.9	9.1	8.7	8.6	8.3
2010	9.0	9.1	9.2	9.0	8.9	
2011	9.3	9.2	9.3	9.1		
2012	9.1	9.2	9.2			
2013	9.2	9.1				
2014	8.9					

Table 2

30° Refer to table 2 to find the total accumulated value for a deposits of 100 made in 2005, 2007, and 2010, and withdrawn at the end of 2011.

31° Refer to table 2 to find the yield in 2014 of an amount deposited in 2004.

1° We explicitly say that the payments start in a year, so the present value is

$$30v + 40v^3 + 55v^5 = 91.76.$$

2° We extend the definition of the present value by using infinite series

$$\sum_{i=1}^{\infty} 35v^i = 35 \sum_{i=1}^{\infty} v^i.$$

We can be sure this will converge, since $v < 1$ and the series is geometric. In fact, it converges to

$$\frac{35}{1-v} = 291.67.$$

3° Assuming you have 100 today, that the person selling you the sequence is trustworthy, and that you don't have any better offers, you should accept the sequence. The present value is $-100 + 0v + 0v^2 + 40v^3 + 50v^4 + 60v^5 + 70v^6 = 3.69$. The present value of not accepting the sequence is 0.

4° We see that the equation of value is

$$1521 = 100 + 100rv + 100r^2v^2 + \cdots$$

$$= 100 \sum_{i=0}^{\infty} (rv)^i,$$

where $r = 1 - 1.1\% = 0.989$. Because we see it has a finite value, we know the series converges. The series is geometric, so we can write

$$1521 = 100 \cdot \frac{1}{1 - rv}$$

and solve for $v = 0.945$.

6° As usual per our convention, we assume that the first payment (of 0) takes place today. The equation of value is

$$188.61 = 0 + 100v + 100v^2.$$

The quadratic formula yields $v = 0.96154\ldots$. We compute $i = v^{-1} - 1 = 0.039998$, approximately 4%.

7° The present value is

$$cv + cv^2 + cv^3 + cv^4 + cv^5 = cv(1 + v + v^2 + v^3 + v^4)$$

$$= cv \sum_{k=0}^{k=4} v^k$$

$$= cv \frac{1 - v^5}{1 - v}$$

so that

$$c = \frac{103(1 - v)}{v(1 - v^5)} = 24.71.$$

8° Recall that under compound interest, $a(10) = (1 + i)^{10}$, so that $1 + i = \sqrt[10]{2.159}$ and $i = 0.08$.

9° Since $a(n) = (1 + i)^n$, we see that

$$\log(1.412) = n \log(1 + i),$$

and

$$n = \frac{\log(1.412)}{1 + i} = 4.$$

10° For compound interest, we have

$$a(n) = (1+i)^n,$$

so that

$$
\begin{aligned}
i_n &= \frac{a(n) - a(n-1)}{a(n-1)} \\
&= \frac{(1+i)^n - (1+i)^{n-1}}{(1+i)^{n-1}} \\
&= \frac{(1+i)^{n-1}\left((1+i) - 1\right)}{(1+i)^{n-1}} \\
&= i.
\end{aligned}
$$

11° A deposit only earns interest for the time it is in the account. The first deposit accumulates to

$$100(1.08)(1.075)(1.07)(1.065),$$

the second deposit accumulates to

$$100(1.075)(1.07)(1.065),$$

and so on. The total accumulated values is the sum of these. But we have a faster way to compute this. Write:

$$1.065 \cdot (50 + 1.07 \cdot (50 + 1.075 \cdot (100 + 1.08 \cdot 100))) = 365.03.$$

12° The accounts earned the same amount of interest at time n. This implies that they had accumulated the same amount at time $n - 1$, since

$$100i = 50i(1+i)^{n-1},$$

so that $2 = (1+i)^{n-1}$, and $n - 1 = \frac{\log 2}{\log 1.065} = 11$ This implies that $n = 12$.

13° We define

$$r(t) = \int_0^t \delta(t) \, dt = \log(0.0125t + e^{0.0125t}),$$

so that

$$a(t) = e^{r(t)} = 0.0125t + e^{0.0125t}.$$

We find the equivalent compound interest rate by solving for i in

$$a(5) = 1.127 = (1+i)^5,$$

so that $i = 2.4\%$.

14° We define

$$r(t) = \int_0^t \delta(t)\, dt = \log(2 - e^{-0.05t}),$$

so that

$$a(t) = e^{r(t)} = 2 - e^{-0.05t}.$$

We recall that

$$i_{10} = \frac{a(10) - a(9)}{a(9)} = \frac{e^{-0.45} - e^{-0.5}}{2 - e^{-0.45}} = 2.3\%.$$

15° Substitute into

$$1 + i = \left(1 + \frac{i^{(12)}}{12}\right)^{12}$$

and solve for $i^{(12)} = 11.39\%$.

16° Substitute into

$$1 + i = \left(1 + \frac{i^{(2)}}{2}\right)^2$$

and solve for $i^{(2)} = 7.84\%$.

17° Substitute into

$$\left(1 + \frac{i^{(4)}}{4}\right)^4 = \left(1 + \frac{i^{(6)}}{6}\right)^6$$

and solve for $i^{(6)} = 8.97\%$.

18° Substitute into

$$\left(1 - \frac{d^{(2)}}{2}\right)^{-2} = \left(1 + \frac{i^{(3)}}{3}\right)^3$$

and solve for $i^{(3)} = 5.11\%$.

19° Substitute into

$$\left(1 - \frac{d^{(2)}}{2}\right)^{-2} = \left(1 + \frac{i^{(12)}}{12}\right)^{12}$$

and solve for $i^{(12)} = 9.24\%$.

20° Each of the terms is an effective m^{th}-ly rate. We can express each in terms of the effective rate i as

$$(1+i)^{\frac{1}{k}} (1+i)^{\frac{1}{2}} = (1+i)^{\frac{1}{6}},$$

so that $k = 3$.

21° Each of the terms is an effective m^{th}-ly rate. We can express each in terms of the effective rate i as

$$(1+i)^{\frac{1}{k}} (1+i)^2 = (1+i)^{\frac{1}{12}},$$

so that $k = -\frac{12}{23}$.

22° As usual, we assume that the first payment occurs today, since we were not told otherwise. Then, the equation of value is

$$40 = 30v^2 + 60v^4$$

This is a quadratic equation in v^2. So we solve for $v^2 = 0.60391$ and $v = 0.77712$. Finally, we find $i = v^{-1} - 1 = 28.7\%$.

23° Use the BAII Plus cash flow functions to find the yield rate. The answer is 32.36%.

24° Solve for j in

$$1 + j = \left(\frac{1525}{1500}\right)\left(\frac{1530}{1500}\right)\left(\frac{1535}{1505}\right)\left(\frac{1550}{1510}\right).$$

The answer is $j = 8.6\%$.

25° Solve for $X = -34.09$ in

$$1.065 = \left(\frac{1100}{1200}\right)\left(\frac{1100}{1100 + X}\right)\left(\frac{1200}{1100 + X}\right).$$

26° We see that

$$I = B - A - \sum_t c_t = 200$$

and that

$$\sum_t (1 - t)c_t = 50 \cdot \frac{1}{12}(10 + 7 + 4 + 1) = 91.667,$$

so that

$$i = \frac{I}{A + \sum_t(1 - t)c_t} = 15.5\%$$

27° We compute

$$\sum_t (1-t)c_t = -600\frac{8.5}{12} + 300\left(\frac{3}{12} + \frac{2}{12} + \frac{1}{12}\right) = -275$$

so that

$$A + \sum_t (1-t)c_t = 725.$$

Since $i = 6.9\%$,

$$0.069 = i = \frac{I}{725},$$

so that $I = 50$. Finally, we solve for B in

$$I = B - A - \sum c_t,$$

to find that $B = 1350$.

28° The equation of value is

$$V = 100 \times 1.088 \times 1.089 \times 1.083 \times 1.084 = 139.10$$

29° The equation of value is

$$V = 1.084 \times 1.083$$
$$\times \left[100 + (1.089 \times (100 + (1.088 \times 100)))\right] = 384.34.$$

30° The equation of value is

$$V = 1.086 \times 1.063 \times \left[100\left(1.065 \times 1.063 \times 1.063\right.\right.$$
$$\left.\left.\times (100 + (1.063 \times 1.062 \times 100)))\right)\right] = 404.38$$

31° $i^{2004+10} = 8.3\%$

3

FINANCIAL INSTRUMENTS

3.1   MOTIVATION

We can define a *financial instrument* as a structured sequence of cash flows. As we saw in 2.2, the value of a series of cash flows varies in time. It should be no surprise that our focus will be understanding how to find the values of financial instruments at any point in time. Luckily, the regularized structure of most financial instruments exposes mathematical regularity. This structure means that we can find mathematically tractible formulas for analyzing the values of these instruments, as opposed to having to use the 'brute-force' method of dealing with sequences of cash flows directly. Moreover, the instruments we will be working with form a 'basis' for expressing a rich variety of structures.

3.2   ANNUITIES

Traditionally, annuities were financial instruments that paid some amount every year. The modern terminology treats an annuities as a financial instrument that pays at regular intervals. Annuities are our most basic structured cashflows.

We will introduce some vocabulary. We see that an annuity is *immediate* if the next payment is due at the end of the current period. We contract this with an annuity *due*, which is an annuity whose next payment is due *now* – that is, at the start of the current period.

Actuarial notation for annuities is somewhat ornate, but we will see some common patterns. In particular, the present value of an annuity is denoted by a, typically decorated with various symbols and variables that tell us about the structure of payments. For example, $a_{\overline{n}|}$ is the present value of a unit annuity immediate, and $\ddot{a}_{\overline{n}|}$ is the present value of a unit annuity due. The accumulated value of an annuity is denoted by s, again, decorated with various symbols and variables. For example, the accumulated value, of a unit annuity immediate is $s_{\overline{n}|}$ and the accumulated value of a unit annuity due is $\ddot{s}_{\overline{n}|}$.

But let's not get ahead of ourselves. You will see all of this notation and what it means in detail, shortly.

3.2.1 *Unit Annuities*

We define a *unit annuity immediate* $a_{\overline{n}|}$ as a sequence of payments of 1, at the end of each of n periods. Of course, the value of a unit annuity depends on the interest rate, and we write $a_{\overline{n}|i}$ if we wish to make this dependence explicit. For a fixed interest rate, finding the present value of the unit annuity immediate is straight forward. We also denote the present value by $a_{\overline{n}|}$, and derive it by

$$a_{\overline{n}|} = v + v^2 + \cdots + v^n$$
$$= v\left(1 + v + \cdots v^{n-1}\right)$$
$$= v\frac{1 - v^n}{1 - v}$$

since the sum is geometric. This expression simplifies to

$$a_{\overline{n}|} = \frac{1 - v^n}{i}.$$

We denote the future value of the n payments at the end of period n by $s_{\overline{n}|}$. The formula can be found very easily. We simply fast-forward n times:

$$s_{\overline{n}|} = \kappa^n a_{\overline{n}|}$$
$$= \kappa^n \frac{1 - v^n}{i}$$
$$= \frac{\kappa^n - 1}{i}.$$

We define the *unit annuity due* as as a sequence of n payments of 1, at the start of each of n periods. We denote the present value of the unit annuity due by $\ddot{a}_{\overline{n}|}$. Since we receive each payment at the start of the period instead of the end, we are effectively fast-fowarding a unit annuity immediate by one period, so that $\ddot{a}_{\overline{n}|} = \kappa a_{\overline{n}|}$ and $a_{\overline{n}|} = v\ddot{a}_{\overline{n}|}$. Similarly, the future value at the beginning of the nth period is denoted $\ddot{s}_{\overline{n}|}$ and is related to $s_{\overline{n}|}$ by $\ddot{s}_{\overline{n}|} = \kappa s_{\overline{n}|}$, so that $s_{\overline{n}|} = v\ddot{s}_{\overline{n}|}$.

An important consequence of these definitions is that any finite constant cash flow can be written as a scaled unit annuity. In particular, consider the sequence that pays P at the end of each period. Then the present value is

$$Pv + Pv^2 + \cdots + Pv^n = P\left(v + v^2 + \cdots + v^n\right)$$
$$= Pa_{\overline{n}|}.$$

We will also consider a class of annuities called the deferred annuities. We will use the unit annuities as examples, but similar results hold for the others. An annuity is *deferred* if it is scheduled to begin some number k of periods in the future.

Consider the unit annuity that pays for n periods, starting at the end of k periods. Then, of course, the first payment occurs at the end of the kth period, so that the equation of value is

$$v^{k+1} + v^{k+2} + \cdots + v^{k+n} = v^k(v + v^2 + \cdots + v^n)$$
$$= v^k a_{\overline{n}|}.$$

This should be expected, since we have to discount each of the payments for the 'extra' k periods. This leads us to the $a_{\overline{n+k}|}$ formula

$$a_{\overline{n+k}|} = a_{\overline{k}|} + v^k a_{\overline{n}|},$$

which follows by adding $a_{\overline{k}|}$ to $v^k a_{\overline{n}|}$.

3.2.2 Combinations of Annuities

Increasing Annuities

We define the *unit increasing annuity* $(Ia)_{\overline{n}|}$ as the n-payment annuity that pays 1 at the end of the first period, 2 at the end of the second, and in general, k at the end of the kth period.

From the definition, we can see that the present value

$$(Ia)_{\overline{n}|} = \sum_{k=1}^{n} k v^k.$$

This sum looks rather opaque, but we can find a big hint by examining a cash flow diagram. We can see that the cash flows represented by the dots on the dashed line can be written as the payments from a unit annuity with n payments. The remaining payments form a deferred increasing unit annuity. In fact, we can see a recurrence relation

$$(Ia)_{\overline{n}|} = a_{\overline{n}|} + v(Ia)_{\overline{n-1}|},$$

That is, that the n-period increasing unit annuity is an n-period unit annuity plus a deferred $(n-1)$-period in-

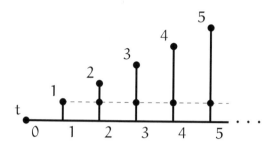

creasing unit annuity. We can remove the recurrence and express this as the sum

$$(Ia)_{\overline{n}} = a_{\overline{n}} + va_{\overline{n-1}} + v^2 a_{\overline{n-2}} + \cdots + v^{n-1} a_{\overline{1}}.$$

This sum is analytically tractable, and the result is

$$(Ia)_{\overline{n}} = \frac{\ddot{a}_{\overline{n}} - nv^n}{i}.$$

We leave the proof as an exercise, since it is good practice for manipulating the annuity formulas.

We denote the value of the increasing unit annuity at the end of the nth period by $(Is)_{\overline{n}}$. We can compute

$$(Is)_{\overline{n}} = \frac{\ddot{s}_{\overline{n}} - n}{i}.$$

As usual, we can define 'due' and accumulation variations for this pattern of payments. The unit increasing annuity due $(I\ddot{a})_{\overline{n}}$ is the annuity that pays k at the beginning of the kth period, for $1 \leq k \leq n$. Of course, we can express this annuity by fast-forwarding $(Ia)_{\overline{n}|}$, so that the present value is

$$(I\ddot{a})_{\overline{n}|} = \kappa \frac{\ddot{a}_{\overline{n}|} - nv^n}{i}.$$

We can define the future value $(I\ddot{s})_{\overline{n}|}$ of the unit increasing annuity due by fast-forwarding $(I\ddot{a})_{\overline{n}|}$ n times, so that

$$(I\ddot{s})_{\overline{n}|} = \kappa \frac{\ddot{s}_{\overline{n}|} - n}{i}.$$

Decreasing Annuities

We define the *unit decreasing annuity immediate* $(Da)_{\overline{n}|}$ as the n payment annuity that pays n at the end of the first period, $n - 1$ at the end of the second, and generally pays $n - k + 1$ at the end of the kth period. As usual, we identify the financial instrument with its present value, and so we denote the present value by $(Da)_{\overline{n}|}$ as well. Although this convention might have seemed unmotivated, it is going to pay off now. Consider the cash flow diagram

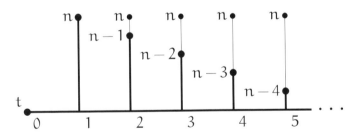

We have superimposed two cash flow diagrams here. First notice that the payments at the top of the diagram are

constantly n, so that the top payments can be represented by an annuity immediate paying n. Second, notice that the difference between the level payments and the decreasing payments are the sequence $\{0, 1, 2, 3, \ldots, n\}$, a sequence with $n + 1$ elements. So we can write

$$n a_{\overline{n+1}|} = (Da)_{\overline{n}|} + v(Ia)_{\overline{n}|}.$$

Notice that we are *not* making a claim about the present values of these annuities.[1] We are making the claim that the sums of the cash flows the decreasing and deferred increasing annuities represent are equal to the cash flows that the level payment annuity represents. This has practical consequences for modelling and problem solving. If a company owns a level payment annuity but it actually wants a decreasing payment annuity, it merely has to sell a deferred increasing payment annuity. Indeed, we model the situation by writing

$$(Da)_{\overline{n}|} = n a_{\overline{n+1}|} - v(Ia)_{\overline{n}|}.$$

We use subtraction – or more accurately, the additive inverse of a financial instrument – to represent selling that financial instrument. Of course, we use positive financial instruments to represent buying or owning. We call financial instruments created by combining other instruments *synthetic*.

As usual, we can define the future value $(Ds)_{\overline{n}|}$ of $(Da)_{\overline{n}|}$ at period n by fast-forwarding the present value n times.

---

1 Of course, the same relationship holds for their present values.

We define the decreasing annuity due $(D\ddot{a})_{\overline{n}|}$ by fast-forwarding $(Da)_{\overline{n}|}$ once, and we can define the future value $(D\ddot{s})_{\overline{n}|}$ of the decreasing annuity due $(D\ddot{s})_{\overline{n}|}$ by fast-forwarding $(D\ddot{a})_{\overline{n}|}$ n times.

Arithmetic Annuities

The arithmetic annuities are generalizations of the increasing and decreasing annuities. The sequence of payments of an arithmetic annuity is an arithmetic sequence. In particular, there exist values P and Q such that the kth payment of the arithmetic annuity is $P + Q(k-1)$. In other words, the first payment is P, and every subsequent payment is Q larger than the previous one. This is non-standard notation, but we like to use $(PQa)_{\overline{n}|}$ to denote the arithmetic annuity immediate. Note that the way we use the notation, the PQ in $(PQa)_{\overline{n}|}$ are there to tell us that the annuity is arithmetic, much like how the I in $(Ia)_{\overline{n}|}$ tells us that the annuity is increasing. They are not variables.

We can see that both $(Ia)_{\overline{n}|}$ and $(Da)_{\overline{n}|}$ are arithmetic annuities. In particular, for $(Ia)_{\overline{n}|}$, $P = 1$ and $Q = 1$. For $(Da)_{\overline{n}|}$, $P = n$ and $Q = -1$.

We can compute the present value of $(PQa)_{\overline{n}|}$ as

$$(PQa)_{\overline{n}|} = Pa_{\overline{n}|} + Q\frac{a_{\overline{n}|} - nv^n}{i}.$$

As usual, we can define the 'due' and accumulation variations for $(PQa)_{\overline{n}|}$ by fast-forwarding an appropriate number of times. In particular,

$$(PQs)_{\overline{n}|} = Ps_{\overline{n}|} + Q\frac{s_{\overline{n}|} - n}{i},$$

$$(PQ\ddot{a})_{\overline{n}|} = P\ddot{a}_{\overline{n}|} + Q\kappa\frac{a_{\overline{n}|} - nv^n}{i},$$

and

$$(PQ\ddot{s})_{\overline{n}|} = P\ddot{s}_{\overline{n}|} + Q\kappa\frac{s_{\overline{n}|} - n}{i}.$$

Geometric Annuities

The geometric annuity immediate $(Ga)_{\overline{n}|}$ is the annuity that pays the sequence of payments

$$\left\{ 1, r, r^2, + \cdots + r^{n-1} \right\},$$

for some real number r. We see that the present value of the kth payment is $v(rv)^{k-1}$, so that the present value of the annuity is

$$(Ga)_{\overline{n}|} = v \sum_{k=1}^{n} (rv)^{k-1}$$

$$= v \sum_{k=0}^{n-1} (rv)^k.$$

And if rv does not equal 1, we can use the geometric sum formula

$$= v\frac{1 - (rv)^n}{1 - rv}.$$

As usual, can define the 'due' and accumulation variations by fast forwarding an appropriate number of periods. In particular,

$$(Gs)_{\overline{n}|} = v\frac{\kappa^n - r^n}{1 - rv},$$
$$(G\ddot{a})_{\overline{n}|} = \frac{1 - (rv)^n}{1 - rv},$$

and

$$(G\ddot{s})_{\overline{n}|} = \frac{\kappa^n - r^n}{1 - rv}.$$

In applications, we frequently see variations of these annuities where we are told that the payment increases by some percentage g. In this cases, we set $r = 1 + g$. Similarly, if the payments decrease by g percent each period, we set $r = 1 - g$.

3.2.3 *Perpetuities*

Many of the payment patterns we have discussed can be extended to infinite sequence of payments. These infinite annuities are called *perpetuities*. For an annuity of 'type' A, we denote the corresponding perpetuity by $A_{\overline{\infty}|}$. So, for example, the level unit perpetuity is denoted by $a_{\overline{\infty}|}$.

We list the present values of the relevant perpetuities without derivation. The derivations are either trivial applications of the geometric sequence or very simple limit arguments.

$$a_{\overline{\infty}|} = \frac{1}{i},$$
$$(PQa)_{\overline{\infty}|} = \frac{P}{i} + \frac{Q}{i^2},$$
$$(Ga)_{\overline{\infty}|} = v\left(\frac{1}{1-rv}\right),$$

if $rv < 1$. Notice that $(PQa)_{\overline{\infty}|}$ subsumes both $(Ia)_{\overline{\infty}|}$ and $(Da)_{\overline{\infty}|}$. We can even define the due variations by fast-forwarding each.

We give one further expression for $(Ga)_{\overline{\infty}|}$. As we have noted, we can express the factor r as $1 + g$, for some g. We can express the present value of a geometric perpetuity as

$$(Ga)_{\overline{\infty}|} = \frac{1}{i-g}.$$

3.2.4 *Stocks*

Many company stocks issue *dividends*, which are payments to shareholders taken from company profits. Perpetuities form a natural way to model these stocks. For the purposes of valuation, buying a share of these companies' stocks amounts to buying the future dividends. And by the no arbitrage principal, the price for a share should be the present value of the future dividends. This is called the *dividend discount model*.

If a company issues a level dividend D at regular intervals, then using a level payment perpetuity model is appropriate. The price of such a stock is

$$\frac{D}{i},$$

where i is an interest rate chosen for the valuation.

If the dividends start at D and increase by some percentage g every period, we can use the *dividend growth model* to find its value. Notice that a share corresponds to a scaled $(Ga)_{\overline{\infty}}$ perpetuity, where $r = 1 + g$, so that the present value of the future dividends is

$$\frac{Dv}{1 - rv} = \frac{D}{i - g}.$$

When evaluating real stocks, the interest rate must be chosen very carefully by considering issues like current yield of Treasury bonds, the company's credit rating, the size and structure of the company's debts, and other relevant factors. For the purposes of Exam FM, this interest rate will either be given, or you will be asked to infer it on the basis of stock valuation models.

3.2.5 *Exercises*

1° Given an effective interest rate of 8%, by how much do the present values of $a_{\overline{10}|}$ and $a_{\overline{11}|}$ differ?

2° Expand the sum and simplify to prove that

$$(Ia)_{\overline{n}|} = \sum_{k=0}^{k=n} v^k a_{\overline{n-k}|} = \frac{\ddot{a}_{\overline{n}|} - nv^n}{i}.$$

3° Expand the sum and simplify to prove that

$$(Ia)_{\overline{n}|} = \sum_{k=1}^{n} kv^k = \frac{\ddot{a}_{\overline{n}|} - nv^n}{i}.$$

4° Prove that

$$(Da)_{\overline{n}|} = \sum_{k=0}^{n} a_{\overline{n}|}.$$

64

5° Expand the sum and simplify to prove that

$$(Da)_{\overline{n}|} = \sum_{k=1}^{n} (n-k+1)v^k = \frac{n - a_{\overline{n}|}}{i}.$$

6° Use the equation

$$(Da)_{\overline{n}|} = na_{\overline{n+1}|} - v(Ia)_{\overline{n}|}.$$

to prove that

$$(Da)_{\overline{n}|} = \frac{n - a_{\overline{n}|}}{i}.$$

7° Prove that

$$(PQa)_{\overline{n}|} = Pa_{\overline{n}|} + Q\frac{a_{\overline{n}|} - nv^n}{i}.$$

8° Write an expression for $(PQs)_{\overline{n}|}$.

9° Given an effective interest rate of 4.5%, what is the future value at time 20 of $(I\ddot{a})_{\overline{10}|}$ followed by $(D\ddot{a})_{\overline{10}|}$?

65

10° Alice buys a 15 year decreasing annuity immediate, at an effective yearly interest rate of 6%. Bob buys a 15 year level payment annuity at the same interest rate and price as Alice. What is the difference between the present values of the fourth payment they receive?

11° Compute $s_{\overline{5n}|j}$, given that $v_i^n = 0.6227497$, $a_{\overline{3n}|i} = 10.8355$, and $j = i + 0.02$.

12° Carol's annuity will begin its monthly payments at the end of the month. The annuity earns interest at a nominal rate of 9%, convertible quarterly. The payments will start at 100 and increase by 5 every month until the end of the first year. The payments will remain constant for 10 years. They will then decline by a level amount each month for 4 months until they reach zero. What is the present value of this annuity?

13° Dave buys a 10 year level payment annuity immediate for 12810. He spends 65% of the income from his annuity and deposits the rest in a savings account earning 2%. Immediately after the third payment, Dave sells the annuity and uses the proceeds and the balance of his savings account to buy a new annuity that matches his spending exactly. What is the length of the new annuity? Assume that the annuities earns an effective rate of interest of 5.5% compounded continuously.

14° Eric's level payment perpetuity pays 100 monthly, and earns a nominal rate of 2.4%, convertible monthly. At the end of the 60th month, Eric decides to sell his perpetuity and purchase a geometric perpetuity that pays 100, 100r, $100r^2$, and so on, and earns a nominal rate discount of 2.634% convertible monthly. What is r?

15° An annuity pays 15 at the beginning of the first month, and increases by 7% each month until the 12th payment. The payment then decreases by 5% each month the 24th payment. If the effective monthly interest rate is 3%, what is the present value?

3.3   DEBT

We are certainly all familiar with the concept of debt. One party, the *lender*, lends the *borrower* an amount of money, called the *principal*, which we denote B_0. The borrower is responsible for paying back the principal, plus interest.

There are several important ways to structure the sequence of payments.

However, all loans share some important terminology, properties, and complications.

The loan balance principle is extremely important. *The balance of a loan after the kth payment is the present value of the remaining payments at time k.* We express this as

$$B_k = \sum_{i=k}^{n} P_{n-i} v^{n-i}.$$

The balance of a loan after the kth payment is the future value of the original balance, minus the future value of the payments up to time k. We express this as

$$B_k = B_0 \kappa^k - \sum_{i=1}^{n-k} P_i \kappa^i.$$

One further complication regarding loans are loan origination fees. We may think of these fees as an additional form of interest, which is charged by discounting the principal by a discount rate d. This charge is usually expressed in terms of 'points', where one point is one percent of the principal. So, for example, a loan of 120, with 16.667% points charged, would give the borrower access to 100, while the borrower would still have to pay for 120 principal.

Each of the different repayment schedules have different notions of how interest is applied, with implications for the total cost of the loan. To help consumers, the United States government has required that many loans must report an *annual percentage rate*, or *APR*, which is the true nominal annual interest rate for the loan.

Loan refinancing is a common option borrowers pursue when interest rates decline. If they find a lender offering a lower interest rate than their current loan costs, they might take out a new loan for the balance of their previous loan. The borrower would then use the new loan to pay for the balance on the old loan. This has the potential to lower costs by significant amounts, especially for longer duration loans.

3.3.1 *Amortization Plans*

Amortization plan loans have several distinguishing features that make them convenient. In an amortization plan, each payment pays for *interest first, and any remaining payment over the interest due is used to pay principal.*

We very often consider level payment amortization loans. We can find the level payment P by considering that the sequence of payments must have the same present value as the principal, under the interest earned by the loan. In particular, for an n term level payment loan for B_0 earning interest i,

$$P = \frac{B_0}{a_{\overline{n}|i}}.$$

We mentioned that each payment pays for interest first, and any remainder over the interest payment is applied to the principal. This means that each subsequent payment will pay for less interest, because the remaining balance will decline after each payment. If we let R_k be the principal paid in the kth period, have the recurrence relations

$$I_k = iB_{k-1},$$
$$R_k = P_k - I_k,$$
$$B_k = (1+i)B_{k-1} - P_k.$$

These recurrence relations hold even for non-level payment loans. They essentially define the amortization plan.

For level payment loans, we can recover the relations

$$R_k = Pv^{n-k+1}$$
$$I_k = P(1 - v^{n-k+1})$$

from the recurrences, using mathematical induction. From the first equation, we see that we can write

$$R_{n+k} = \kappa^n R_k.$$

We call the quantities I_k and R_k the amount of *amortization of interest and principal*, respectively.

For level payments, we can calculate the loan balance at any time k with the basic loan balance principals. Recall that the loan balance at time k is the present value of its remaining payments. For a level payment loan, we have

$$B_k = Pa_{\overline{n-k}|}.$$

Similarly, the loan balance at time k is the accumulated value of the original balance minus the future value of the remaining payments. For a level payment loan, we have

$$B_k = \kappa^k B_0 - P s_{\overline{n-k}|}.$$

One natural question arises. What happens if a person misses a payment, or makes a partial payment? In this situation, the lender increases the loan balance by the amount of the unpaid interest. The recurrence relations take care of this for us automatically, since, in particular

$$B_k = (1+i)B_{k-1} - P_k.$$

3.3.2 *Installment Plans*

In *installment* repayment of loans, a fixed amount of principal is repaid in each payment, in addition to interest on the remaining balance. For an installment plan with N scheduled payments and principal B_0, the principal paid in the kth payment is

$$R_k = \frac{B_0}{N}.$$

The balance immediately after the kth payment is

$$B_k = B_0 \left(1 - \frac{k-1}{N}\right).$$

This means that the interest paid in the kth payment is

$$I_k = iB_{k-1} = iB_0 \left(1 - \frac{k-1}{N}\right),$$

and that the total payment in the kth period is

$$R_k + I_k = \frac{B_0}{N}(1 + i(N - k + 1)),$$

which we recognize as a $(PQa)_{\overline{N}|j}$ annuity with

$$P = B_0 \left(\frac{1}{N} + i \right)$$

and

$$Q = -\frac{iB_0}{N}.$$

In principle, we can find the yield for the installment plan by solving for j in the equation of value

$$B_0 = B_0 \left(\frac{1}{N} + i \right) a_{\overline{N}|j} - \frac{iB_0}{N} \frac{a_{\overline{N}|j} - Nv^N}{j}.$$

Installment plan loans are easy to describe, but certain aspects are difficult to analyze. Computing the APR of an installment plan loan can be difficult, since it can require solving high degree polynomials with varying coefficients. However, these problems can be solved by using the cash-flow worksheet in your BAII Plus calculator. There is a variation of the installment plan which can be handled analytically. We might consider an installment plan with $i = 0$ but with loan origination fees. These loans have fixed payments, so their equations of value are just geometric sums.

For the purposes of the exam, it is far more important to understand the structure of the installment plan payment schedule than to memorize the equation of value.

3.3.3 Sinking Fund Plans

A *sinking fund plan* is a loan plan that requires the borrower to pay interest each month, and also make deposits into an interest bearing account, called a *sinking fund*, with the purposes of paying the principal at the end of the term. Because the borrower only pays for interest, the borrower must pay the entire principal at the end of the term of the loan. This loan payment schedule has a higher total interest payment than an amortization plan schedule with the same quoted interest rate, but if the return on the interest bearing fund is high enough, the sinking fund plan can have a lower total cost.

We can calculate the interest paid each period as $I = iB_0$. Since the borrower must pay B_0 after n periods, we see that the borrower's deposit must be D in

$$B_0 = Ds_{\overline{n}},$$

so that

$$D = \frac{B_0}{s_{\overline{n}j}},$$

where j is the rate at which the fund earns interest. The borrowers total payment must be

$$B_0 \left(\frac{1}{s_{\overline{n}j}} + i \right) = I + D.$$

The balance of the sinking fund at time k is

$$Ds_{\overline{k}|j} = B_0 \frac{s_{\overline{k}|j}}{s_{\overline{n}|j}}.$$

We use the balance of the sinking fund to find the principal 'paid' in any period. In particular, the principal paid in the kth period is the amount accumulated in the sinking fund between k and $k-1$. We note that this is

$$D(1+j)^{k-1}.$$

This is a payment only in an accounting sense. The funds are not transferred to the borrower, but the funds are set aside and considered a payment for the purposes of taxation. Once we have the principal paid in a period, we can also calculate the interest paid. We call this the *net interest*, since it is the difference between the nominal rate of the loan and the interest earned by the sinking fund. The net interest is

$$B_0(\frac{1}{s_{\overline{n}|j}} + i) - D(1+j)^{k-1} = I - jB_0\frac{s_{\overline{k}|j}}{s_{\overline{n}|j}}.$$

3.3.4 *Bonds*

A business or other large organization may issue a bond when it needs to raise funds. A *bond* is a special kind of loan, which represents a fraction of the total amount the company borrows. For example, if a national government needs to borrow a billion dollars, it might have difficulty finding a counter-party with that much money available at an attractive interest rate. To avoid this difficulty, the government might write $100,000$ loans with standardized terms, for 10000 each. This standardization of the terms of a bond issue means that each bond becomes a fungible good and can trade on an open market.

The *par value*, or *face value*, F of a bond is a nominal amount for the bond. The *redemption value* C is the amount due at the *redemption date* – when the bond expires. Typically, the redemption value is the face value, but it can differ. *If we are not explicitly told that they differ, we may assume they are equal.* A *coupon* is a payment made at regular intervals. It is calculated by multiplying the *coupon rate* r for the bond by the face value. Coupons are typically paid semi-anunally (every 6 months), and the coupon rate r is typically reported as a nominal semi-annual interest rate which must be converted to an effective rate. As usual for financial instruments, the price for a bond is the present value of its remaining payments. Suppose that a bond pays a coupon rate r every period for n periods. At the end of the n years, the bond expires and the redemption value is paid as well. The equation of value for this situation is

$$V = (Fr)a_{\overline{n}|i} + Cv_i^n.$$

This is the basic equation for bond pricing.

We must explain where the yield rate i comes from. It is each purchaser's 'personal' interest rate. As we discussed in 2.1, the interest rate i represents the purchaser's preferences regarding the time value of money. In modern economic terms, this preference is set by comparing the risk of the the bond issuer defaulting to the *risk-free rate* – the rate i that high quality government bonds yield on the open market. Because it is believed that strong governments with fiat currencies will never allow their bonds to default, their bonds are said to face no credit risk. These bonds do face other kinds of risk, such as the risk of inflation and reinvestment risk. However, interpreting the risk free rate as a measurement of risk is not straight-forward. In any case, the risk-free rate is the *least* a bond – or any other investment – can earn, because every other investment faces the same systemic risks, in addition to the risk of default.

Bond Premiums

A bond is said to sell at a *premium*, or be a *premium bond*, if the coupon rate is greater than the yield rate. Similarly, a bond is said to sell at a *discount*, or be a *discount bond*, if the coupon rate is lower than the yield rate. *Under the assumption that* $F = C$, the premium-discount formula lets us examine the effects on price of relative changes in r and i, since

$$V = F + F(r - i)a_{\overline{n}|}.$$

Indeed, we see that if $r = i$, then the bond should sell exactly at face value. The coupons will be exactly enough to pay the interest on the loan balance, which will be paid in a lump sum at the end of the life of the bond.

If a bond sells at a premium, it means that the coupons pay for more than just interest on the principal. In fact, the coupons pay for the premium paid over the face value when the bond was purchased. We call this the *amortization of bond premiums*. The amount of the premium paid in the kth period is

$$F(r-i)v^{n-k+1}.$$

If a bond sells at a discount, it means that the coupons do not pay the whole amount of the interest on the principal. The bond's owner pays for the discounted price at the time of purchase by taking smaller interest payments than the prevailing market yield rate. Again, the amount of discount paid in the kth period is

$$F(r-i)v^{n-k+1}.$$

From these expressions, we can readily see that the amount of premium or discount amortized in the $(m+k)^{th}$ period is

$$\kappa^m F(r-i)v^{n-k+1}.$$

In a sense, this is an accounting issue, instead of a financing or economic issue. There are many equivalent ways in which the premium or discount for a bond can be paid for. However, a standardized method is required in order to comply with regulations and for the purposes of taxation.

Callable Bonds

We have seen that the price of bonds depends both on the coupon they pay in addition to their yield. Bonds can sell for more than their face value if the coupon is high enough. Bonds can sell for less than their face value if they yield is high enough. But let us consider this situation from the bond issuer's point of view. The issuer will clearly want to pay as little as it can to secure the financing it needs. Once a bond has been issued, there is no going back. The issuer received what buyers thought of as the present value for the bond when it was first auctioned by the issuer. In doing so, the issuer has locked in the yield rate it has to pay for the life of the bond, *regardless of what it sells for after the initial auction*.

But what if prevailing attitudes towards interest rates change after the bond has been issued? If yield rates decline, it would be beneficial to 'cancel' the old bond and issue a new bond at the lower yield rate. This is not a possibility for typical bonds, but a *callable bond* grants the issuer the option to 'cancel' the bond after a fixed number of periods, but before the redemption date.

A callable bond lowers the issuer's interest rate risk, but increases the bondholder's interest rate risk. With a non-callable bond, the bondholder would find itself in a position where it has locked in yield rates higher than it can get now. Calling the bond means that the issuer 'unlocks' the yield, and that the bond holder would have to reinvest the re-demption value at a lower prevailing yield rate. To address this issue, issuers sometimes offer higher redemption values if the bond is called before the redemption date.

Pricing callable bonds is not a straight-forward matter. In effect, we must use the *expected value principle* to find the *fair*, or *actuarial*, value of the bond. We would weigh the prices at different interest rates by the probability that these interest rates will occur, keeping in mind that there is a ceiling on the price due to the issuer's ability to call the bond. More refined models would treat interest rates as a random walk, and consider the present value of the bond as interest rates change in time. For the purposes of Exam FM, we should be able to use the bond pricing formulas under different circumstances. For example, we might be told that a bond is priced to yield i if it gets called in the 10th year. In this case, we would use the basic pricing formula, using i as our yield rate, and 10 years as our time.

Prices for Fractional Periods

The most basic pricing principal tells us that the price of an asset is the present value of the future cash flows generated by the asset. For bonds, this means the coupons and the redemption of the par value. But what happens if we buy a bond in between coupon dates? We can find a very good approximation of the price.

The basic principal for dealing with a fractional period is that the previous owner owns the interest accumulated up to the date of the sale. But by buying the bond, we receive the full coupon payment. So we must pay for the fraction that the previous owner has earned, at the time of the sale. Typically, simple interest is used. Indeed, let B_k be the book value of the bond after the kth coupon. Then, if t is the fraction of the period the previous owner owned the bond, the sale price is

$$B_k + (Fr)t.$$

This price is truly approximate, because it does not fully take the time-value of all the payments into account. In particular, to find the true present value of the bond at the time of the sale, we should be fast-forwarding all of the cash flows by t. But the approximation is commonly used in practice.

Problems involving fractional periods will typically tell us which days of the year the coupon dates and date of sale are. t is the fraction of the period that the previous owner held the bond. So we calculate t by finding the length of time beyond the last coupon date the previous owner held the bond, and dividing by the length of the period.

Zero-Coupon Bonds

Because of the theoretical importance of bonds with zero-coupon rate, we define the *unit zero-coupon bond* $Z_{0,T}$ as the bond with par value 1 payable at time T. For convenience, we will typically assume continous compound interest when dealing with zero-coupon bonds. Of course, at a force of interest δ, the present value is

$$Z_{0,T} = e^{-\delta T}.$$

We denote the future value of $Z_{0,T}$ at time t by $Z_{t,T}$. The future value is $Z_{t,T} = e^{-\delta(T-t)}$.

The unit zero-coupon bond is essentially a unit cash flow at time T. We can scale zero-coupon bonds. The bond $\alpha Z_{0,T}$ pays α at time T.

The theory of annuities can, in principle, be built up using portfolios of scaled unit zero-coupon bonds at redeemable at different times. But the real importance of the unit zero-coupon bond is that it represents the simplest loan possible – a loan with a single lump sum payment of principal and interest.

The yield on a zero-coupon bond is called the *spot rate*. The United States Treasury does not issue zero-coupon bonds, but zero-coupon bonds can be created by separating the coupon payments and the principal payment of a coupon-bearing Treasury bond and selling them separately. These zero-coupon bonds are called *Treasury strips*, and the yield on Treasury strips is called the *Treasury spot rate*. These zero-coupon bonds are sold by government bond dealers, and are effectively backed by the full faith and credit of the United States government. For all intents and purposes, the Treasury spot rate is the risk-free rate.

Spot rates are denoted by s_n, where n is the number of years until the bond matures. The functional relationship between n and s_n is called the *term structure of interest rates* or the *yield curve*.

The shape of the yield curve is theoretically important. If it is upward sloping, then short term interest rates are expected to rise. If it is downward sloping, short term interest rates are expected to decrease. A flat yield curve indicates that interest rates are not expected to change much.

We can explain this with the no-arbitrage principle, since we can synthetically create a zero-coupon bond as a sequence of zero-coupon bonds. In particular:

$$Z_{0,T} = \left(e^{-r(T-t)} \cdot Z_{0,T-t}\right) \triangleright Z_{T-t,T},$$

where the $\triangleright$ means "followed by" – we hold the bond

$$\left(e^{-r(T-t)} \cdot Z_{0,T-t}\right)$$

until it matures at time $T - t$, and use the proceeds of $e^{r(T-t)}$ to purchase $Z_{T-t,T}$.

The no-arbitrage principle tells us that the yield for the single bond on the left side must be the same as the yield from both bonds on the right side combined. This means that

$$(1 + s_n)^n = (1 + s_{n-k})^{n-k}(1 + i_{n-k,n})^k,$$

for any n and k, where $i_{n-k,n}$ is the interest rate earned by a k year zero-coupon bond starting at $n - k$. We call these *forward rates*. For problem solving purposes, we will mostly be interested in forward rates of the form $i_{n,n+1}$, for which we can calculate

$$1 + i_{n,n+1} = \frac{(1 + s_{n+1})^{n+1}}{(1 + s_n)^n}$$

and

$$(1 + s_n)^n = (1 + i_{0,1})(1 + i_{1,2}) \cdots (1 + i_{n-1,n}).$$

Forward rates are important in many ways. They represent the theoretical forward prices for interest rate forwards. As such, they are market-based estimates of interest rates in the future.

Similarly, spot rates are important as well. They give us market-based estimates of interest rates at varying terms of maturity, and let us calculate more accurate present values for sequences of cash flows than the constant interest models we have previously considered. Indeed, for a sequence of cash flows $\{c_n\}$, we define the present value of $\{c_n\}$ by

$$\sum_n \frac{c_n}{(1+s_n)^n}.$$

3.3.5 *Exercises*

16° Candice pays 691.58 per month for a 15 year loan that charges a nominal rate of 3%. What is the original principal?

17° Charles pays 819.25 per month for a 10 year loan for 75000. What is effective yearly interest rate?

18° Chistopher has a 30 year loan for 200, 000. The loan charges a nominal rate of $i^{(12)} = 9.8\%$. What is Chistopher's monthly payment?

19° Danielle has a 20 year loan that charges a nominal rate $i^{(12)} = 5.8\%$ for 100000. Danielle paid 1200 per month for seven years. What is her balance after seven years?

20° Jacob has a loan for 100000 that charges a nominal rate of 6.4%, convertible monthly. Jacob's monthly loan payment is 865.62. How many years long is the loan?

21° Jerry has a 10 year, 20,000 loan that costs a nominal rate of 7.5%, convertible monthly. How much principal did Jerry pay in his 60th payment?

22° Joan enters into a 300,000, 30 year mortgage with a nominal interest rate of 9.4%, and monthly payments. She is also charged a 4 point loan origination fee. What is her APR?

23° Prove that, for a sinking fund plan,

$$B_0 \left(\frac{1}{s_{\overline{n}|j}} + i \right) - D(1+j)^{k-1} = I - jB_0 \frac{s_{\overline{k}|j}}{s_{\overline{n}|j}}.$$

24° Find the level sinking fund deposit D for a 10 year loan for 10,000, if the sinking fund earns 3%.

25° The amount of principal paid into a sinking fund in th 10th period is half the principal paid in the 18th. What interest rate does the sinking fund earn?

26° What is the principal paid in the 10th period for a 1000 loan on a 12 period installment plan, with 9% interest?

27° What is the interest paid in the 10th period for a 10,000 loan on a 25 period installment plan, with 9% interest?

28° Fred buys a flat screen television for 1000, on an installment plan with 12 level monthly payments and no interest, but is charged 16.6667 points. What is his total payment on the loan?

29° Earlier today, Ginger bought a large sectional sofa for 2400, on an installment plan, with 6 monthly payments an interest rate reported as a nominal 14% compounded monthly. The first payment is due today. What is her APR?

30° Find the price of a $1000 par value 10 year bond with a coupon rate of 5%, convertible semi-annually, priced to yield 8%.

31° A 5000 dollar par value zero-coupon bond expires in N years. It is priced to yield 2.5%, at a price of 3717.779. What is N?

32° Find the price of a 1000 face value 25 year bond with a coupon rate of 7% convertible semi-annually, when priced to yield 7% convertible semi-annually.

33° A 10 year, 1000 dollar par value bond with coupon rate $r^{(2)} = 8\%$ and yield rate $i^{(2)} = 7\%$ costs 1025.13. What is the redemption value?

34° A 1000 par value 5 year bond is priced at 1044.33, to yield 5.5%, convertible semi-annually. Coupons are disbursed semi-annually. What is the nominal coupon rate, convertible semi-annually?

35° A bond has a face value of 1000 and pays a semiannual coupon of 50. The bond yields a nominal rate of 6% convertible semiannually. How much premium is paid in the 5th period?

36° It is found that the bond premium amortized in the first period is 18.32. If the nominal yield rate convertible semi-annually is 9%, how much premium was amortized in the 12th period?

37° A 20 year bond has a nominal coupon rate of 9% convertible semiannually, and is priced at auction to yield a nominal rate of 7% convertible semiannually, if held to expiration. The bond can be called at any time after the tenth period. What is the maximum yield a bondholder can expect?

38° A 1000 par value bond with semi-annual coupons of 25 is priced to yield $i^{(2)} = 4.5\%$. Jason bought the bond with 5.5 periods left before the redemption date. How much did Jason pay?

39° Use the table of spot rates to find the present value for the sequence of cash flows {500, 500, 500, 10500} starting at the end of the year.

Term	Spot Rate
1	6.5%
2	6.8%
3	7.1%
4	7.4%

40° Use the table of forward rates to calculate the price of a 1000 par value bond paying a nominal 9% coupon rate convertible semi-annually and maturing in 3 years.

n	$i_{n,n+1}$
0	5.5%
1	5.0%
2	4.5%

3.4 SOLUTIONS

1° We can compute

$$a_{\overline{10}|} = \frac{1 - v^{10}}{i}$$
$$= 6.71008$$

and

$$a_{\overline{11}|} = \frac{1 - v^{11}}{i}$$
$$= 7.13896,$$

so that the difference is 0.42888. Or we can compute $a_{\overline{11}|} - a_{\overline{10}|}$ by noting that $a_{\overline{11}|} = a_{\overline{10}|} + v^{11}$, so that their difference is $v^{11} = 0.42888$.

$7°$ To begin, note that the kth cash flow has present value

$$[P + Q(k-1)]\, v^k.$$

By collecting all of the "P terms" and "Q terms" into sums, we have

$$P\left[\sum_{k=1}^{n} v^k\right] + Q\left[\sum_{k=1}^{n} (k-1)v^k\right].$$

The sum on the left is clearly a scaled level annuity. We can re-index the latter sum

$$\sum_{j=0}^{n} jv^{j+1} = v\sum_{j=0}^{n-1} jv^j.$$

We note that the sum is now

$$v(Ia)_{\overline{n-1}|} = v\frac{\ddot{a}_{\overline{n-1}|} - (n-1)v^{n-1}}{i},$$

$$= \frac{a_{\overline{n-1}|} - (n-1)v^n}{i}$$

$$= \frac{a_{\overline{n-1}|} + v^n - v^n - (n-1)v^n}{i}$$

$$= \frac{a_{\overline{n}|} - nv^n}{i}.$$

This concludes the proof, since we can substitute into

$$Pa_{\overline{n}|} + Qv\frac{\ddot{a}_{\overline{n-1}|} - (n-1)v^{n-1}}{i}$$

to yield

$$Pa_{\overline{n}|} + Q\frac{a_{\overline{n}|} - nv^n}{i}.$$

8° We must merely fast-forward $(PQa)_{\overline{n}|}$ n times. The expression is

$$Ps_{\overline{n}|} + Q\frac{s_{\overline{n}|} - n}{i}.$$

9° Perhaps the simplest way to solve this problem is to compute the present value

$$(I\ddot{a})_{\overline{10}|} + v^{10}(D\ddot{a})_{\overline{10}|}$$

and fast-forward 20 times

$$\kappa^{20}\left((I\ddot{a})_{\overline{10|}} + v^{10}(D\ddot{a})_{\overline{10|}}\right).$$

10° We begin by writing the equation of value

$$(Da)_{\overline{n|}} = Pa_{\overline{n|}},$$

so that

$$P = \frac{n - a_{\overline{n|}}}{1 - v^n}.$$

This is a straight-forward computation, whose numerical solution is $P = 9.074$, and so the present value of Bob's fourth payment is 7.1874. Alice's fourth payment is 12, and its present value is 9.5051. Their difference is 2.32.

11° We write

$$10.8355 = a_{\overline{3n|}}$$
$$= a_{\overline{n|}} + v^n a_{\overline{n|}} + v^{2n} a_{\overline{n|}}$$
$$= a_{\overline{n|}}\left(1 + v^n + v^{2n}\right),$$

so that

$$a_{\overline{n|}} = \frac{10.8355}{1 + v^n + v^{2n}}$$
$$= 5.38928.$$

We are now in a position to solve for i by simplifying

$$i = \frac{1 - v^n}{5.38928}$$
$$i = 0.07,$$

so that

$$j = 0.08.$$

We solve for n by taking logarithms

$$\log v^n = \log 0.6227$$
$$= n \log v$$

so that

$$n = \frac{\log 0.6227}{\log \left(1.07^{-1}\right)}$$
$$= 7.$$

Finally, we write

$$s_{\overline{5n}|j} = \frac{\kappa_j^{35} - 1}{j}$$
$$= 172.317.$$

12° Note that the interest rate is nominally 9%, convertible quarterly. We will have to convert it to an effective monthly rate. So we solve for i in

$$\left(1 + \frac{i^{(4)}}{4}\right)^4 = (1 + i)^{12}$$

and find that $i = 0.74444\%$. We express the present value of the annuity by

$$(PQa)_{\overline{12}|i} + 155v^{12}a_{\overline{120}|i} + 31v^{132}(Da)_{\overline{4}|i},$$

where $P = 100$ and $Q = 5$. We suggest drawing a cash flow diagram that includes the transitions from one kind of annuity to another. Once the problem is set up, this is a routine, if lengthy, calculator problem. Remember to use the effective monthly interest rate. The total present value is 12794.18.

13° To start, we calculate the level payment. The present value is 12810, so the equation of value is

$$12810 = Pa_{\overline{10}|}$$
$$P = \frac{12810}{a_{\overline{10}|}}$$
$$P = 1699.474.$$

We see that Dave spends $0.65P = 1104.658$ and deposits $0.35P = 594.816$ in a savings account at the end of every year for three years. The present value of his savings account in three years is the accumulated value $0.35Ps_{\overline{3}|2\%} = 1820.375$. The price of the annuity he sold is the present value at the time of sale of the remaining payments: $Pa_{\overline{7}|5.5\%} = 9658.056$. So Dave can afford to pay 11478.431 for his new level payment annuity. We can calculate the length of the new annuity by solving for n in $11478.431 = 1104.658a_{\overline{n}|5.5\%}$, which can be done most easily using the BAII Plus time value functions. The answer is $n = 15.83$.

$14°$ First we note that we have been given a nominal interest rate, convertible monthly. We see that the effective monthly interest rate is $i = \frac{i^{(12)}}{12}$. The present value of the perpetuity at the time of sale is the present value of its future payments. We write the equation of value

$$V = 100a_{\overline{\infty}|}$$

and simplify

$$= \frac{100}{0.002}$$
$$= 50,000.$$

This means Eric can pay $50,000$ to purchase the new perpetuity. By examining the payments closely, we see that Eric buys $100(Ga)_{\overline{\infty}|}$. We write the equation of value

$$50,000 = 100(Ga)_{\overline{\infty}|}$$
$$= 100v\frac{1}{1-rv}.$$

We must make a brief detour to find v. We are told that this perpetuity earns a nominal rate of *discount* of $d^{(12)} = 2.634\%$, convertible monthly, so that the monthly effective rate is $d = 0.002195\%$, and $v = 1 - d = 0.997804$. We now solve for r in the equation of value, so that $r = 1.002$.

$15°$ We find drawing a cash flow diagram useful for this kind of problem, especially for the times around transitions from one kind of annuity to another. We see that this is a geometric annuity, where $r = 1.07$, followed by another geometric annuity, where $r = \rho = 0.95$. We write the equation of value

$$V = 15(G\ddot{a})^{7\%}_{\overline{12}|i} + 15r^{11}v^{12}(G\ddot{a})^{-5\%}_{\overline{12}|i}.$$

We like to use 'ρ' as our alternate growth multiplier when 'r' is already in use. We can expand this to

$$15\frac{1-(rv)^{12}}{1-rv} + 15r^{11}v^{12}\frac{1-(\rho v)^{12}}{1-\rho v}.$$

We see that the present value of the first annuity is 223.87. The present value of the deferred annuity is 177.05. The total value is 400.94.

16° Use the BAII Plus time value functions to find the principal, which is 100000.

17° Use the BAII Plus time value functions to find the monthly effective interest rate, which is 0.47%. Calculate the yearly effective rate by solving for i in $(1 + i) = 1.0047^{12}$, so that $i = 5.8\%$.

18° Use the BAII Plus time value functions to find the monthly payment, which is 1725.66.

19° Use the BAII Plus time value functions to find balance, which is 25960.60.

20° Use the BAII Plus time value functions to find the term, in months, as 180. This is 15 years.

21° Use the BAII Plus time value functions to calculate the monthly payment $P = 237.40$. Then use the formula

$$R_k = Pv^{n-k+1}$$

to find that $R_{60} = 162.34$.

22° We begin by computing the monthly payment for the loan. We see that the loan is for 30 years, or 360 months. We see that the nominal interest rate is 9.4%, so that the monthly effective rate is 0.783%. Joan's loan is for $300,000$, and her balance after the last payment is 0. We use the BAII Plus time value functions to calculate that her monthly payment is 2501. Joan, however, was charged 4 points. This means that Joan's loan paid for a 4% fee, so that Joan only received $288,000$. Effectively, she took out a $288,000$ loan but is paying for a $300,000$ loan. Her payments, number of payments, interest rate, and final balance all remain the same. We use the BAII Plus time value functions to calculate the interest charged for a $288,000$ loan with 360 monthly payments of 2501 as 10.1%.

24° The sinking fund must accumulate $10,000$ in 10 years. We solve for D in
$$10000 = Ds_{\overline{10}|3\%},$$
so that $D = 872.31$.

25° We see that
$$2D(1+j)^{10-1} = D(1+j)^{18-1},$$
so that $(1+j)^8 = 2$. We see that $j = 9.1\%$.

26° The principal paid in any period in this installment plan is
$$\frac{B_0}{N} = \frac{1000}{12} = 83.33.$$

27° We are asked for the quantity $I_{10} = iB_9$. Since it is an installment loan, we see that the principal paid in each payment is $B_0/N = 10000/25 = 400$, so that the balance after the 9th payment is $B_9 = 10000 - 3600 = 6400$. The interest paid in the 10th period is $iB_9 = 576$. Of course, we could have used the formula
$$I_k = iB_0\left(1 - \frac{k-1}{N}\right) = 0.09 \cdot 10000\left(1 - \frac{9}{25}\right) = 576.$$

28° Since Fred is charged points, we see that he must borrow an amount greater than 1000 in order to have 1000 available to pay for the television. In fact, he must borrow $\frac{1000}{1-d}$, where $d = 0.166667$. Of course, we see that his balance is 1200, and since he is charged no interest, his total payment is 1200.

29° We see that Ginger pays 400 of principal with each payment. We convert her yearly nominal interest rate $i^{(12)}$ to an effective monthly rate $i = 1.166\%$. Her total monthly payments, including interest, are the sequence

$$\{428, 423.33, 418.67, 414, 409.33, 404.67\}.$$

Recall that the payments start today. The equation of value is

$$2400 = 428 + 423.33v + 418.67v^2$$
$$+ 414.00v^3 + 409.33v^4 + 404.67v^5$$

This is a quintic polynomial equation, and as we know, there is no general algebraic method to solve this equation. We use the BAII Plus cash flow and internal rate of return tools to calculate that the loan costs an effective rate of 1.97% per month. The nominal annual interest rate, then, is 23.6%.

34° We use the basic pricing formula

$$1044.33 = 1000r a_{\overline{10}|i} + 1000v^{10},$$

so that

$$r = \frac{1.04433 - v^{10}}{a_{\overline{10}|}} = 0.0275.$$

This is the effective coupon rate, so we must convert it to a nominal semi-annual coupon rate. We fine $r^{(2)} = 5.5\%$.

35° We use the premium amortization formula to find the premium paid in the 5th period.

$$F(r - i)v^{n-k+1} = 1000(0.05 - 0.03)v^{16} = 7.87$$

36° We see that

$$18.32 = F(r - i)v^{n-1+1} = F(r - i)v^{n}.$$

The amount of premium paid for in the 12th period is

$$F(r - i)v^{n-12+1} = F(r - i)v^{n-11} = \kappa^{11}F(r - i)v^{n} = 29.73.$$

37° *Note that the phrasing of this question is tricky.* We must calculate the highest yield the bondholder can expect. This is the lowest yield the bondholder can earn with this bond. If he 'expects' a higher yield, his expectations will be frustrated when the bond is called. The present value of the cashflows generated if the bond is not called is

$$(Fr)a_{\overline{40}|3.5\%} + Fv^{40} = F\left(0.045a_{\overline{40}|3.5\%} + v^{40}\right) = 1.21355F.$$

On the other hand, the present value of the cashflows the bond generates if called at the end of the tenth period is

$$(Fr)a_{\overline{10}|j} + Fv^{10}.$$

Since the bond was bought for 1.21355F, we find the yield by solving for j in

$$1.21355 = ra_{\overline{10}|j} + v^{10},$$

so that j is approximately 2.11%. Then, the nominal yield convertible semiannually is 4.22%.

38° This is a fractional period problem. Jason bought the bond with 5.5 periods remaining. We calculate the book value of the bond immediately after the last coupon before the sale. We see that this is

$$25a_{\overline{5}|} + 1000v^5 = 894.71.$$

The previous owner owned the bond for another half a period, and the interest accrued during that period belongs to her. By default, we use a simple interest approximation, so that Jason paid $894.71 + 0.5 \times 25 = 907.21$.

39° The present value using these interest rates is calculated as

$$\frac{500}{1.065} + \frac{500}{1.068^2} + \frac{500}{1.071^3} + \frac{10500}{1.074^4} = 9207.$$

40° We must calculate spot rates to use in our present value calculation. Recall that we compute

$$(1 + s_n)^n = (1 + i_{0,1})(1 + i_{1,2}) \cdots (1 + i_{n-1,n}).$$

So we calculate

n	$i_{n,n+1}$	s_{n+1}
0	5.5%	5.5%
1	5.0%	5.25%
2	4.5%	4.87%

We are now in a position to calculate the present value

$$V = \frac{45}{1.055^{\frac{1}{2}}} + \frac{45}{1.055} + \frac{45}{1.0525^{\frac{3}{2}}} + \frac{45}{1.0525^2} + \frac{45}{1.0487^{\frac{5}{2}}} + \frac{1045}{1.0487^3},$$

so that $V = 1115$.

4

DERIVATIVE INSTRUMENTS

4.1 MOTIVATION

A *derivative* is a contract whose value is 'derived from' the value of some underlying good. That is the folk-lore, at least, but we think it misses a vital point. Derivatives allow us to fine-tune our exposure to risk, by allowing us to buy and sell *rates of change* of cost or payoff functions with respect to the price of the underlying good. Derivative contracts allow us to literally buy and sell derivatives, in the sense of calculus.

We will introduce several derivative contracts, including the forward contract, the swap, and the options contract. All derivative contracts share certain features. Each one has an underlying good, which we denote by S. We denote the price for S at time t by S_t. All derivative contracts have an expiration date, which we denote by T. Every derivative contract has an expiration date, as well.

Derivative contracts, as a category, are very flexible. Businesses often get together to negotiate a customized derivative contract that works for them. These are called *over the counter* contracts. For example, forward contracts and swaps are often written in this way. Other contracts are standardized, specifying an underlying good, a quantity, an expiration date, and so on. By standardizing the terms of the contracts, it becomes possible to create fluid markets for these contracts. For example, futures contracts are, in essense, standardized, exchange traded forward contracts.

4.2 FORWARD CONTRACTS

A forward is an arrangement to make a transaction at an agreed upon price, at some time in the future. Forwards are some of the most common business arrangements. Businesses use forwards to 'lock in' prices. Instead of worrying about unfavorable price movements, a business can agree on a price today, for a transaction in the future.

Forwards can be agreed upon informally, such as when you order food from a restaurant for delivery. You agree on a price when you call, and pay it when the food arives. Forwards can also be codified into contracts. Futures contracts are standardized, market traded forward contracts. Forward contracts can also be created by businesses negotiating directly with each other. These are called *over the counter* contracts. For the purposes of valuation, all of these kinds of arrangements can be treated the same way.[1]

We denote the forward contract to purchase an underlying asset S at time T by $\mathcal{F}_t^T$. As usual, we denote its present value by $\mathcal{F}_t^T$, as well.

We define $F_{t,T}$ as the price to be paid for S at time T, given that the contract was entered at time t. We denote the value of the underlying asset S at time t by S_t.

4.2.1 *Forward Pricing*

Pricing for forward contracts is done entirely by the no-arbitrage principal. Suppose that the underlying accumulates value at a continuous rate r. Then, its accumulated value at time T is $S_0 e^{rT}$. By the no-arbitrage principle, this is the price one must agree to pay at time T in a forward arrangement. If $F_{0,T}$ is higher than this, you can profit by entering a forward arrangement to sell S at time T while simultaneously buying a bond that yields r until time T. Then, at time T, you can sell the bond, purchase the underlying for S_T, and sell it for $F_{0,T}$, netting a profit of $F_{0,T} - S_T$. If $F_{0,T}$ is lower than $S_0 e^{rT}$, then you can profit by entering a forward agreement to buy S at time T, while simultaneously buying S at time 0. By time T, the underlying should be

---

1 We purposefully ignore the risk of default. Informal agreements are the riskiest. Formal contracts have some risk of default, which is measured by the counter-parties' credit rating. Futures contracts have virtually no default risk for the counter-parties, because of the mechanics of how the contracts are settled. These issues are beyond the scope of this book.

worth $S_T = S_0 e^{rT}$, so one can sell S for S_T and buy S for the agreed upon forward price, netting a profit of $S_T - F_{0,T}$.

This model can be expanded to include underlying goods that do not accumulate value in time. We can do this with the *cost of carry* model. The cost of carry is the total cost to hold a good for some length of time. For example, one might face transportation, financing, storage, and insurance costs. If we express this cost as a fraction c of the spot price, the cost of carry model tells us that $F_{0,T} = S_0(1 + c)^T$. Of course, we can turn the effective rate c into a force of interest r to recover the previous formula. An empirical estimate of r can be derived as

$$ r = \frac{1}{T} \log \left(\frac{F_{0,T}}{S_0} \right), $$

which in this context is called the *implied repo rate*. The rate r must be chosen after serious and careful consideration of circumstance and available information about the underlying asset and the markets in which it is traded.

As usual, this issue is beyond the scope of this book. For the purposes of Exam FM, the rates will either be given to you or you will infer a rate using the pricing models. However, it should be noted that the kinds of arbitrage we used only exist to the degree that our assumptions agree with reality.

We will develop pricing formulas for more specific situations. The general principle is that the price for a forward contract should be the present value, at time T, of the future cash flows generated by the underlying.

Consider the situation where we would like to buy stock that yields quarterly dividends $\{d_t\}$. The price S_0 includes the value of the dividends. If we enter a forward contract to buy a share at time $T = 1$ year, we would take possession of the share after four of the dividends were disbursed. Their value would not belong to us. In that case, we would pay

$$e^{rT}\left(S_0 - \sum_{t<T} d_t e^{-rt}\right) = S_0 e^{rT} - \sum_{t<T} d_t e^{r(T-t)}.$$

The case in which dividends are disbursed continously uses similar reasoning. Suppose that the dividend rate is δ. Then the forward price is
$$S_0 e^{(r-\delta)T}.$$
Whatever the forward price, can see that
$$\mathcal{F}_0^T = F_{0,T} e^{-rT}.$$

This is also called the *prepaid forward price*, denoted $F_{0,T}^P$, since it is the amount that would be paid at time $t = 0$, if the buyer and seller agreed to settle the payment then instead of at time T.

4.2.2 *Forward Payoffs, Profits, and Strategies*

We briefly discussed the payoff of entering into a forward contract when we discussed pricing. We will discuss these issues in depth.

Consider an underlying asset S currently priced at S_0. Under our assumptions above, the expectation is that the price

S_T will be $S_0 e^{rT}$. However, there is a risk that $S_T \neq S_0 e^{rT}$. Indeed, this is exactly the kind of risk that entering into forward contracts eliminates. The seller of the underlying good might be worried that prices will fall by time T. The buyer of the underlying good is worried that prices will rise. By entering into a forward contract, both the buyer and seller eliminate that risk by settling on a price today.

The *payoff*, or intrinsic value, of a long forward contract is $S_T - F_{0,T}$. If the spot price S_T is higher than the forward price $F_{0,T}$, the buyer will 'win' $S_T - F_{0,T}$. By taking on the forward contract, the buyer would have ensured she paid less than the spot price. If the spot price S_T is lower than $F_{0,T}$, the buyer will have to pay $F_{0,T} - S_T$ more than the spot price. She will 'lose' $F_{0,T} - S_T$. Equivalently, she will 'win' the negative amount $S_T - F_{0,T}$. By similar reasoning, the payoff for a short forward contract is $F_{0,T} - S_T$. Notice that the seller 'wins' what the buyer 'loses', and vice-versa.[2]

The *profit* for a forward contract is the same as the payoff, since there are no costs incurred to enter the contract.

Consider a wheat farmer who is concerned about price fluctuations. He will have 50,000 bushels ready for delivery in 3 months. His total cost of production is 1.7 per bushel of wheat. The spot price for wheat is 2.00 per bushel. Suppose that the prevailing continuous interest rate is 4%. Then a 3 month forward contract would have a forward price of

---

2 This makes the forward markets a zero-sum game – but only if we ignore the value created by allowing buyers and sellers to lower the variance of the prices they face.

S_T	Unhedged Profit	$F_{0,T} - S_T$	Hedged Profit
1.50	−0.2	0.52	0.32
1.60	−0.1	0.42	0.32
1.70	0	0.32	0.32
1.80	0.10	0.22	0.32
1.90	0.20	0.12	0.32
2.00	0.30	0.02	0.32
2.10	0.40	−0.08	0.32
2.20	0.50	−0.18	0.32

Table 3: The farmer's unhedged profit, profit due to the forward contract, and total hedged profit, at various prices. Notice that the hedged profit is the sum of the unhedged profit and the profit due to the forward.

$F_{0,0.25} = 2.0e^{0.04 \cdot 0.25} = 2.0201$. If the farmer entered into a forward contract for 50,000 bushels, his total profit per bushel would be 0.32, for a total profit of 16005. Note that this is not the profit from the forward contract. His hedged profit is the profit from the forward contract plus his profit from an unhedged position, as we can see in table 3.

The farmer is probably much more concerned about earning profit from his farming activities than the profit his forward earns. By entering into a forward contract, the farmer has guaranteed that he will have 0.32 profit per bushel. From a more analytical perspective, the hedged profit has zero variance, which removes the inherent uncertainty of the unhedged position. A risk-averse firm would prefer to lock in reasonable profits rather than risk losing money.

We can also consider a more nuanced approach to using forward contracts. Instead of entering into a contract to sell all of its wheat, the farmer can enter into a forward contract to sell a fraction of its wheat, and plan on selling the rest at the spot price.

The *hedge ratio* h the fraction of the producer's inventory that is part of a forward contract obligation. Let us denote the per unit cost of production as C, and the total number of units produced by N. Then the profit earned by entering into forward contracts for a fraction h of the inventory and selling the rest at the spot price is

$$P = N\left[h\left(F_{0,T} - C\right) + (1-h)\left(S_T - C\right)\right].$$

Now, let us consider the derivative

$$\frac{\partial P}{\partial S_T} = (1-h)NS_T.$$

We can see that entering into forwards contracts allows us to control the rate of change at which the profit changes in response to changes in the underlying price. We can make that rate of change 0 by setting $h = 1$, as we have seen in our previous examples. We can make the rate of change 1, by not hedging at all. We can choose any number in between.[3]

---

3 We can even choose numbers outside of the interval $[0, 1]$, but that would take us outside the realm of hedging, into *speculation*.

4.2.3 *Synthetic Relations*

We have already seen that forwards can be used to hedge against unfavorable price changes, by locking in a sale price in advance. We can consider a wider class of possibilities by introducing the synthetic forward relation.

Suppose that an asset currently costs S_0. Then we can see that the forward price for the asset is $S_0 e^{rT}$. Instead of entering into a forward contract, we will instead borrow S_0 at an interest rate r. We will purchase S with the loan, now, at a price S_0, and pay back the loan at time T, for $S_0 e^{rT}$. It is easy to see that this series of transactions has the same payoff as entering into long forward contract. Indeed, if S_T is greater than $F_{0,T} = S_0 e^{rT}$, then we come out ahead by the amount $S_T - F_{0,T}$. If S_T is less than $F_{0,T}$, we lose an amount $F_{0,T} - S_T$.

The *synthetic forward relation* tells us that for an underlying asset S,

$$\mathcal{F}_t^T = S_t - S_t Z_{0,T}$$

We are literally saying that we can construct a long forward by selling a zero-coupon bond for S_t – that is, borrowing until time T – and buying the underlying S at time t.

One interesting feature of this equation is that 'regular arithmetic' works. Indeed, we can construct a synthetic stock by adding the bond $S_t Z_{t,T}$ to both sides of the equation.

$$S_t = \mathcal{F}_t^T + S_t Z_{0,T}$$

In words, we enter into a forward contract, and pay S_t for a zero-coupon bond earning r, so that by time T, we have earned $S_t e^{r(T-t)} = F_{t,T}$. We can then use the proceeds of the bond to fulfill our contractual obligation to buy the bond.

Similarly, we can construct a zero coupon bond by buying the underlying at time t and entering into a forward contract to sell it at time T, since

$$S_t Z_{0,T} = S_t - \mathcal{F}_t^T.$$

The synthetic forward relation is essential to Exam FM.

4.2.4 *Futures Markets*

Futures markets engage in the trading of standardized forward contracts, called *futures contracts*. Futures contracts are not as flexible as general purpose forward contracts. The quantity of the underlying good, expiration, and other important contract terms are set by the futures market exchange instead of by businesses negotiating terms appropriate for their situation. This standardization means that futures contracts are best suited for fungible goods, such as grain, metals, and money. Futures contracts may not be as flexible as forward contracts in general, but the relative inflexibility has benefits. The standardization of contract terms effectively makes the contracts themselves fungible goods. Transaction costs for forward contracts are much lower, since the terms of the contract have already been decided. The mechanics behind futures markets virtually eliminate counter-party, or credit, risk. This further lowers transaction costs, because market participants can forego a costly investigation into the counter-party's ability to fulfill their obligations.

Futures contract holders face no counter-party risk because of the system of margin and marking-to-market. *Margin* is a certain amount futures exchanges require market participants to deposit into a special margin account for the purposes of covering any losses. At the close of each trading day, the value of each contract is recorded, and net changes to each participant are withdrawn or deposited to the margin account, to or from the counter-party's margin account. In other words, price changes on the contract are settled on the day they occur, by withdrawing funds *already* in the counter-party's margin account.

Suppose that party A entered into a 100 long futures contract this morning. If the price of the contract increases to 105 this afternoon, he notionally has to pay 105 for the underlying good. On the other hand, because of daily settlement, he receives 5 in his account at the end of the day. This means that his net obligation is still only 100. Similarly, if the price drops to 90 the next day, 15 is withdrawn from his margin account. A notionally has to pay 90 for the underlying, but has lost 10 from his margin account.

Each futures contract has an *initial margin* requirement. This is the amount that must be deposited in the margin account in order to enter a futures position. The *maintenence margin* is the minimum amount required in the margin account in order to maintain an open futures position. If losses bring the margin account balance below the maintenance margin, the trader is required to deposit enough funds to bring the account balance back to the initial margin requirement. This is known as a *margin call*. Since an open futures position gets closed if margin requirements are not fulfilled, margin lowers the risk of default by removing people who are unlikely to be able to meet their contractual obligations before they actually cause any financial damage.

Margin is not the only practice that help reduce default risk. One common practice in futures markets is entering into *offsetting positions* to effectively cancel a contract. If a long contract holder enters into a short contract, the obligation to buy and the obligation to sell effectively 'cancel out', and the holder is left with no net position. For various logisitical reasons, most futures contract positions are closed by offsetting positions. Physical delivery of the underlying good is rarely demanded. Because of margin requirements, a contract position that is closed with an offsetting position cannot default. Indeed, the only way that a position can default is if the long holds the contract until expiration and either the long or the short are unable to deliver. This happens infrequently enough that the futures market itself is able to provide *performance guarantees*. The futures market clearinghouse acts as a market maker and handles the logistics of daily settlement. It does this by being the counterparty to both the buyer and the seller of the underlying, so that it has no net position in the market. In the case that either the buyer or seller default, the clearinghouse makes sure that the other party gets what they expected.

4.2.5 Exercises

$1°$ An annuity due earns a nominal rate of 9% compounded quarterly and pays 15 per quarter for three years. What is the one year forward price for the annuity?

$2°$ Calculate the forward price $F_{0,T}$ for 5,000 bushels of wheat for delivery in 6 months if the current price is 6.90 per bushel, and the risk-free rate is 4%.

$3°$ It is known that the forward price $F_{0,1}$ for the underlying S is 1100, and that the spot price is $S_0 = 1033$. What is the continuous interest rate?

$4°$ A gold mining company has production costs of 640,000 per kilogram of gold. 10 kilograms will be ready in 6 months. The company enters into a forward agreement to sell 5 kilograms, and plans to sell the rest at the spot price S_T. What is the company's total profit if $S_T = 630,000$ and $r = 0.12$?

5° A widget manufacturing company has per unit production costs of 0.35. The current wholesale price for widgets is 0.42. The company enters into a forward agreement to sell some of their widgets in 6 months. The spot price at time T is 0.48, and the average per unit profit is 0.09786. If $r = 0.04$, what fraction of widgets were sold at the spot price?

6° A gas company enters into a 6 month forward contract to buy half the natural gas it needs. It finances the forward obligation with a zero-coupon bond. The current market price is 1778 per ton. The company paid an average price of 1864 per ton at. If the forward earned a profit of 118, what was the yield rate on the bond?

7° A futures contract for pork bellies has an initial margin requirement of 350 and a maintenance margin requirement of 200. Ian opens a long position to pay 800. The closing prices, starting on his first day, are given in the table

Day	Close
1	760
2	510
3	520
4	360
5	600
6	800
7	1000

Assuming Ian deposits the minimum margin necessary, what is the ratio of margin earned to margin deposits?

4.3 SWAPS

A *swap* is an agreement to exchange periodic payments. In an *interest rate swap*, one side pays a fixed amount, while the other side pays an amount that depends on the value of a debt instrument. The party that pays the fixed amount is called the *pay-fixed* side, while the party that pays a varying amount is called the *receive-fixed* side. The two parties are more generally called *counterparties*.

A swap contract requires agreement about the number and timing of the payments. This is called the *swap term* or *swap tenor*. The swap contract requires agreement about the size of the *notional* or *nominal principal*, which is a nominal amount used to calculate payments. The pay-fixed side pays fixed-interest on the nominal principal, while the receive-fixed side pays variable interest on the nominal principal. In a typical interest rate swap, one counterparty must pay the other counter party more, depending on whether the fixed interest rate is higher or lower than the variable rate. Instead of both making payments, the party with the larger payment just makes a payment of the difference between the two. In other words, the parties typically make *net payments*.

We can model a swap contract in several ways. Indeed, we can construct synthetic swap contracts using the same models. We will briefly discuss a few, in order to gain intuition. Perhaps the conceptually simplest way to model a swap contract is by thinking of the counterparties both making loans to each other. Since the nominal principals are the same size, they do not actually 'transfer' the principal. But they both make interest payments for the term of the swap. At the end of the swap, they both nominally pay the principal and close their positions. But again, since each borrowed the same amount from the other, no cash flow actually occurs to 'pay' the principal. We can see that the fixed-pay side 'borrows' at a fixed interest rate, while the other side 'borrows' at a variable rate.

Thinking of a swap contract in terms of partially offsetting loans between the counterparties is especially natural for *foreign exchange swaps*. In foreign exchange swaps, the principals are not principals in name alone, but they are actually exchanged. In these, one party actually has a need for a foreign currency, so it really does receive foreign currency from a counterparty. In exchange, it loans its domestic currency to the counterparty, who also has a need for foreign (to them) currency. The swap payments are based on the relative values of the currencies. At the end of the foreign exchange swap, the counterparties return the principals.[4]

---

4 These so-called *back-to-back* loans were the birth place of the modern swap. English companies hoped to escape foreign exchange controls set by the British government. They found their loophole by loaning

We can also model swap contracts in terms of sequences of offsetting zero-coupon bonds or offsetting annuities. Perhaps the most important theoretical model is to treat a swap contract as a portfolio of forward contracts on the same underlying, expiring at different times. Each swap payment is represented by a forward contract to trade a debt instrument at a fixed price. Of course, the payoff of the forward contract is the difference between the agreed upon price and the actual market price when the forward contract expires. The payoff the swap is the sum of the differences between the fixed price and the actual market prices when the payments are due. The price of a swap is the fixed interest rate that makes the expected payoff and profit 0. Let $F_{0,t}$ be the forward price for a forward contract expiring at time t, and let v_n be

$$v_n = \frac{1}{1 + s_n},$$

so that v_n is the discount factor derived from the n-year spot rate. Suppose that a swap has n payments, and let r be the fixed price. Then the payoff for the swap is

$$\sum_{i=1}^{n} (r - F_{0,t_i}) v_i^i.$$

British Pounds to other companies in exchange for loans of the currency they needed.

Notice that this is the net present value of the swap payments for the receive fixed side. If the expected payoff is 0, we can write

$$\sum_{i=1}^{n} (r - F_{0,t_i}) v_i^i = 0$$

and solve for r by separating the terms and factoring r. We separate the terms:

$$\sum_{i=1}^{n} r v_i^i = \sum_{i=1}^{n} F_{0,t_i} v_i^i,$$

and factor r, so that

$$r = \frac{\displaystyle\sum_{i=1}^{n} F_{0,t_i} v_i^i}{\displaystyle\sum_{i=1}^{n} v_i^i}.$$

We call this the *general swap pricing formula*.

Given a yield curve and swap term n, we can calculate the *swap spread* as $r - s_n$. The swap spread represents the cost of short term borrowing over the spot rate s_n. A swap dealer might set swap prices by setting the swap spread for different categories of credit risk, so that a riskier counterparty would have to pay a higher swap spread than a less risky counterparty.

We can also consider *deferred swaps*, which are swaps that are set to begin their payments some number of periods k in the future. We price these using the same present value reasoning. In particular, we modify the general swap rate formula to begin in k periods, and end in $n + k$ periods, for an n period swap:

$$ r = \frac{\sum_{i=k}^{n+k} F_{0,t_i} v_i^i}{\sum_{i=k}^{n+k} v_i^i}. $$

In a *prepaid swap*, the pay-fixed party pays the present value of the fixed payments. The received-fixed side then makes payments at the variable rate at the scheduled times. We can use present value reasoning to find the pre-payment. We solve for r in the general swap pricing formula, and then calculate

$$ r \left[\sum_{i=1}^{n} v_i^i \right] $$

to discount the fixed payments. On the other hand, we can see that this quantity is exactly

$$ \sum_{i=1}^{n} F_{0,t_i} v_i^i $$

by multiplying each side of the general swap pricing formula by the sum of the discount factors.

We have a further formula for pricing interest rate swaps given a yield curve. For an n-period interest rate swap, we can write

$$r = \frac{1 - v_n^n}{\sum_{i=1}^n v_i^i}.$$

We have discussed models and pricing for swaps, but we have not discussed why somebody would enter into a swap. The most important reason is hedging. In particular, just as a forward contract allows parties to lock in a price, so does the swap. Indeed, the swap allows the parties to lock in a price over multiple periods, within a single contract. This has the potential to lower the transaction costs over entering multiple separate forward contracts. Commodity swaps are commonly used for this purpose in, for example, the oil industry.

Swap contracts allow companies to turn variable rate debt into fixed rate debt, and vice-versa. For example, a company can effectively turn a variable interest rate loan into a fixed rate loan by entering into the pay-fixed side of a swap. It would receive a variable payment, depending on the market price of interest. It can then apply this payment to its variable loan. In other words, it pays a fixed cost instead of a variable cost. This has applications beyond mere hedging. For example, a bank borrows money from its depositors at a variable rate, but might want to make long term, fixed rate mortgage loans. Without swaps, financing its interest payments to its depositors would be more difficult and expensive.

As you will see in the exercises, swap problems are somewhat complicated and time-consuming. We suggest using
table-based problem solving, which will help organize and
clarify. There are many possibilities for complications. We
will focus on interest rate swap problems.

Calculating the payoff for a swap is straight-forward, once
we have calculated the swap rate r. We simply examine the
observed spot price at the end of the relevant period, and
find their difference.

Calculating the profit for a swap can be more involved. In
particular, for an interest rate swap, by observing the price
of a one-period zero coupon bond, we have observed new
information regarding interest rates than the information
seen when the swap rate was originally calculated. When
we calculate the present value of the swap payments, we
should use this new information. We must be aware of
which 'stage' of the process we are in when we solve a profit
problem. Finding the swap rate cannot use information
'from the future', because those prices are not yet known.
Forward prices are estimates for the future spot prices. This
complication might or might not exist for a commodity
swap.

4.3.1 *Exercises*

8° Use the data below to find the swap rate.

n	Spot Rate	Forward Rate
1	3.61%	3.61%
2	3.27%	2.94%
3	2.97%	2.37%

9° Use the data below to find the swap rate.

n	Spot Rate	Forward Rate
1	7.40%	7.40%
2	6.78%	6.16%
3	6.21%	5.08%

10° Use the data below to find the swap rate.

n	Spot Rate	Forward Rate
1	3.19%	3.19%
2	3.48%	3.78%
3	3.81%	4.46%

11° Use the data below to find the swap rate.

n	Spot Rate
1	9.70%
2	10.0%
3	10.3%

12° Use the data below to find the swap rate.

n	Forward Rate
1	11.7%
2	12.6%
3	13.5%

13° Macaulayco enters into the pay-fixed side of an interest rate swap based on the spot rates in the table below. What is the nominal principal if Macaulayco earned a total profit of 1863.76?

n	Spot Rate	Observed Rate
1	11.7%	12.4%
2	12.2%	12.6%
3	12.6%	14.2%

4.4 OPTIONS

As we saw in 2.1, the ability to make choices is valuable. An *option* is a contract that gives its owner the right, but not the obligation, to perform a specific action before or at a predetermined time. A *call option* gives the owner the right to purchase an asset at a price specified in the contract. A *put option* gives the owner the right to sell an asset at a price specified in the contract. In either case, the previously agreed upon price is called the *exercise* or *strike* price. The exercise price is often denoted by X or K. We adopt the convention that K and K′ are exercise prices, with K < K′.

As usual, will adopt the convention of notationally identifying an asset and its present value. We denote a call option with exercise price K and expiration T by $\mathcal{C}(K, T)$. Similarly, we denote a put option with exercise price K and expiration T by $\mathcal{P}(K, T)$. We denote the value of an option at time t with a subscript t, like $\mathcal{P}_t(K, T)$ or $\mathcal{C}_t(K, T)$.

We must make an important point here. A trader who owns an option has rights, not obligations. But a trader who sells an option has obligations. If a trader sells a call option, then if the option is exercised, she is obligated to sell the underlying asset at the exercise price. Selling an option is sometimes known as *writing* an option.[5]

A *European option* stipulates that the right granted by the contract can only be exercised on the expiration date. A *Bermudan option* stipulates that the right can only be exercised on certain dates. An *American option* stipulates that the right can be exercised on any date before expiration.

If the owner of an American option does not wish to exercise the option before expiration, he is exactly as well

---

5 Options clearing houses keep track of each trader's obligations. If a trader buys an option $\mathcal{P}(K, T)$ for S_T and then sells an option $\mathcal{P}(K, T)$ for S_T, then she has effectively sold the option she had previously bought, even though she is strictly speaking, writing a new contract. The obligations from selling are effectively transferred to the writer of her long put option, so that her long and short options "cancel out."

off as he would have been if he had a European option. We would expect an American option to be more valuable than a European option, simply because it affords greater flexibility. On the other hand, options are typically not exercised. Most traders enter a position and then sell ownership of the option before it expires. In other words, option obligations are typically settled by cash payments at the market value of the option. This practice is common, but exposes a trader to risk. If a trader cannot find a trading partner to offset a profitable position, the trader would have to exercise the option in order to realize the profits earned. This could require seeking short-term financing on short notice. That is hardly convenient and can entail large opportunity costs. In growing recognition of this fact, several options markets have begun issuing *cash-settled* options, which require cash payments of the option's payoff instead of physical delivery. In any event, the practice of offsetting options positions tends to nullify the differences in value between American and European options. Indeed, there should be no difference at all for cash-settled options. We will focus exclusively on European options.

4.4.1 *Payoffs and Profits*

Options are contingent contracts, and their payoffs depend on the value of the underlying asset. The payoff at expiration for the long call option $\mathcal{C}(K, T)$ is $\mathcal{C}(K, T) = \max(0, S_T - K)$, where S_T denotes the value of the underlying asset at expiration. We can see why. If $S_T \leq K$ at expiration, then there is no purpose in paying K to buy S_T. One could simply pay S_T instead. In this case, the option is effectively worthless. On the other hand, if $S_T > K$, then purchasing S_T at the price K yields savings of $S_T - K$.

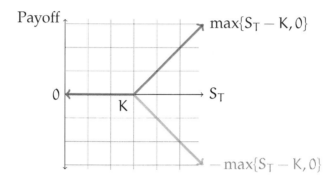

Figure 1: The payoff for a call option at expiration is a function of the underlying price S_T. The dark graph is the payoff for the long call and the light graph is the payoff for the short call. Notice that they agree where S_T is less than K.

The payoff at expiration for the long put option $\mathcal{P}(K, T)$ is $\max(0, K - S_T)$. If $S_T \geq K$, there is no purpose in selling S_T for K. One could simply sell it for S_T. If $S_T < K$, then selling S_T for K makes sense. One earns an extra $K - S_T$ over the market value of S_T. It is worth noting that the payoff for a short option contract is the opposite of the payoff for

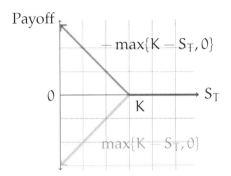

Figure 2: The payoff for a put option at expiration is a function of the underlying price S_T. The dark graph is the payoff for the long put and the light graph is the payoff for the short put. Notice that the graphs agree where S_T is greater than K.

the corresponding long option contract. In particular, the payoff for $-\mathcal{C}(K, T)$ is

$$-\max(0, S_T - K),$$

and the payoff for $-\mathcal{P}(K, T)$ is

$$-\max(0, K - S_T).$$

We also see this in the figures 1 and 2.

Much has been said about how this makes the options market a zero-sum game. However, those analyses ignore the value created by allowing people to lower the variance of the value of their holdings or increase it drastically. In particular, there is value in having predictable cash flows, because they allow businesses to create robust, realistic plans.

Notice that a short option has, at best, a payoff of 0, and at worst, a negative payoff. But the payoff does not include the *premium*, which is the price the long option holder paid for the option. By the no-arbitrage principle, this should be the expected present value of the option – in other words, $\mathcal{P}(K, T)$ or $\mathcal{C}(K, T)$.

We say that an option contract is *in-the-money* if the payoff of exercising the option is positive. For a call option, this occurs when $S_t > K$. For a put, it occurs when $S_t < K$. We say that the contract is *out-of-the-money* if exercising the option has a negative payoff. For a call option, this occurs when $S_t < K$, and for a put, it occurs when $S_T > K$. We say that the contract is *at-the-money* if $S_t = K$.

We summarize the profits in table 4. We can see, again, that the profit of a long option contract is the negative of the profit of the short option contract. And we see that the profit for long contracts is always the payoff minus the premium, whereas the profit for short contracts is the premium minus the payoff. These relationships are important to remember, especially for practical problem solving.

4.4.2   *Put-Call Parity*

Consider the payoffs of $-\mathcal{P}(K, T)$ and $\mathcal{C}(K, T)$. The payoff for the short put option is 0 when S_T is greater than K. The payoff for the long call option is 0 when S_T is less than K.

132

Option	Profit
Long Call	$\max\{S_T - K, 0\} - \mathcal{C}(K, T)e^{rT}$
Long Put	$\max\{K - S_T, 0\} - \mathcal{P}(K, T)e^{rT}$
Short Call	$\mathcal{C}(K, T)e^{rT} - \max\{S_T - K, 0\}$
Short Put	$\mathcal{P}(K, T)e^{rT} - \max\{K - S_T, 0\}$

Table 4: Option contract profits.

Aside from when $S_T = K$, each is 0 exactly when the other one is not. This means that if we create a position consisting of a long call and a short put, the payoff is exactly the non-zero parts of the payoffs of the component parts, since the zero-payoff parts contribute nothing to the payoff. In particular, we can see that the payoff for $\mathcal{C}(K, T) - \mathcal{P}(K, T)$ is $S_T - K$, so that the combination $\mathcal{C}(K, T) - \mathcal{P}(K, T)$ is a synthetic forward contract with $F_{0,T} = K$. Refer to figure 3. We can substitute into the synthetic forward relation, so that at time 0,

$$\mathcal{C}(K, T) - \mathcal{P}(K, T) = S_0 - KZ_{0,T}.$$

We can generalize the put-call parity relation to any time t, like so

$$\mathcal{C}_t(K, T) - \mathcal{P}_t(K, T) = S_t - KZ_{t,T}.$$

The *put-call parity* relation is important because it relates the prices of bonds, underlying assets, calls and puts. It allows us to find the price of one in terms of the others. More importantly, it opens the possibility of using no-arbitrage pricing for complex synthetic instruments.

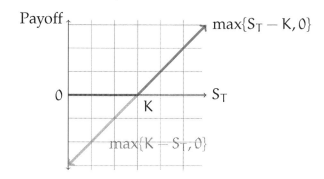

Figure 3: The payoff for a long call and a short put combined is the diagonal line. The payoff intersects the payoff axis at $-K$. The diagonal line is also the payoff for a forward contract to purchase S for K at time T.

4.4.3   *Synthetics and Strategies*

Floor

A *floor* is the most basic of hedging positions. A floor allows us to own an asset, and protect us against the possibility of the asset losing value, while still allowing it to appreciate in value.

We can construct a floor with

$$S + \mathcal{P}(K, T),$$

which, by put-call parity, is equivalent to the position

$$KZ_{0,T} + \mathcal{C}(K, T).$$

We will focus our analysis on the $S + \mathcal{P}(K, T)$ position. Consider the payoff diagram 4. We see that the payoff is effectively the payoff of a call option, translated by K. Indeed, the payoff function is

$$K + \min\{S_T - K, 0\} = \min\{S_T, K\},$$

and the profit is

$$\min\{S_T, K\} - \mathcal{P}(K, T) - S_0 e^{rT}.$$

One interesting observation is that the put option acts as *insurance* on the value of the underlying. The put option ensures that the total position will have a value of at least K, in the event that the value of the underlying decreases below K. The put option plays the role of an insurance policy. Indeed, we can model insurance policies as 'conditional' put options. A typical insurance policy is more restrictive than the general put options we have considered, insofar as an insurance policy only covers the underlying against losses due to *specific* perils. But, given an insured value of S_0, an insurance policy with deductible d has the same payoff as a put option on S with exercise price $S_0 - d$. We can see this, since if a loss of X occurs, then $S_T = S_0 - X$. Since the policy's payoff is $\max(X - d, 0) = \max(S_0 - S_T - d, 0) = \max(S_0 - d - S_T)$, we see that this is the payoff of a put

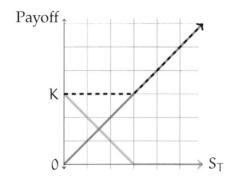

Figure 4: The floor payoff. The put is the light gray graph, and the underlying is the dark line. Their sum is the dashed graph. Notice how this is effectively the payoff of a call option, translated by K.

option with exercise price $K = S_0 - d$. Put in words, an insurance policy is a put option to sell damaged portions of our property for their insured value, minus the deductible.

Covered Call

The *covered call* consists of the position $S - \mathcal{C}(K, T)$. The purpose of the covered call is to attempt to profit from periods of below average volatility. If a trader does not expect that the price of the underlying will increase dramatically, the trader might write call options, in the expectation that they will not be exercised. This means that the trader would keep the premium *and* the underlying.

The covered call is less risky than what we might call a *naked call*, which is just the position $-\mathcal{C}(K, T)$. The naked call faces unbounded risk, since the price of the underlying can rise without limit. If the price S_T is greater than the exercise price, the call will be exercised, and the trader will have to buy a share at S_T in order to sell it at a loss for K. With the covered call, at least, the trader will already own the asset to sell.

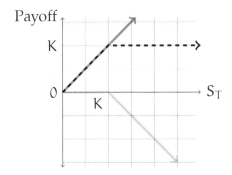

Figure 5: The payoff for the covered call. The covered call lets you earn profits in times when the underlying price is stable. The light gray graph is the payoff for the naked call. Notice that the writer of a naked call faces the risk of unbounded losses.

Bull Spread

The bull spread is a position designed to profit from increasing prices of the underlying, but at a lower cost than a call. It consists of

$$\mathcal{C}(K, T) - \mathcal{C}(K', T).$$

We see that as long as $S_T < K'$, the bull spread has the same payoff as $\mathcal{C}(K, T)$. The difference is that by selling $\mathcal{C}(K', T)$, we earn a premium, but also limit the potential payoff to K'. The payoff for the bull spread is

$$\begin{cases} 0 & \text{if } S_T \leq K, \\ S_T - K & \text{if } K \leq S_T \leq K', \\ K' - K & \text{if } K' \leq S_T. \end{cases}$$

Bear Spread

A bear spread is the short bull spread. It is designed to profit from falling stock prices. It can be constructed as $\mathcal{C}(K', T) - \mathcal{C}(K, T)$. The payoff for the bear spread is

$$\begin{cases} 0 & \text{if } S_T < K, \\ K - S_T & \text{if } K \leq S_T \leq K', \\ K - K' & \text{if } K' \leq S_T, \end{cases}$$

which is graphed in figure 7. We see that the payoff is at best 0. However, this does not consider the premium earned by selling a call option. Figure 8 shows the profit diagrams for both the bull and bear spread.

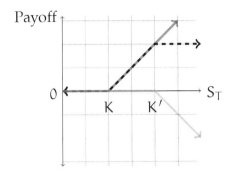

Figure 6: The bull spread payoff. The bull spread hedges against declining values at a lower cost than a call, since we earn a call premium. In exchange, we limit our profit potential.

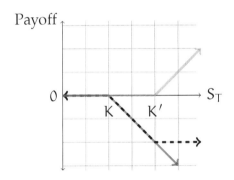

Figure 7: The bear spread payoff.

Box Spread

A box spread consists of the position

$$(\mathcal{P}(K,T) - \mathcal{C}(K,T)) - (\mathcal{P}(K',T) - \mathcal{C}(K',T)),$$

139

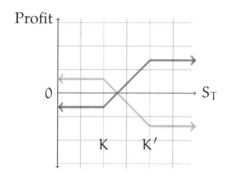

Figure 8: Bull and bear spread profits.

which we recognize as a combination of synthetic forward contracts. With the box spread, we construct a long forward contract to buy at the price K, and construct a short forward contract to sell at the higher price K'.

Because we must pay the premiums today, and get a payment of $K' - K$ at time T, this position is effectively a zero-coupon bond, and, by the no-arbitrage principle, entering the position must cost $(K' - K)e^{-rT}$.

Collar

A collar consists of the position $\mathcal{P}(K, T) - \mathcal{C}(K', T)$. The collar has similar payoffs to a short forward contract, as we can see in the payoff diagram. Unlike the forward contract, we are not contractually obligated to sell at expiration if $K < S_T < K'$. We call the difference between K and K' the *collar width*. We can think of a synthetic forward contract as a collar with zero collar width.

A collar is most interesting when used for the purposes of hedging. As we have seen, the value of the position $S + \mathcal{P}(K, T)$ cannot decrease beyond K. By adding a short call to the position, we lower the cost of the position but, in exchange, make it impossible for the value of the position to increase beyond K'. If the price of the underlying increases beyond K', the call will be exercised, and we will be left with a worthless put and K'. In other words, a collared stock behaves like a bull spread combined with $K \cdot Z_{0,T}$. Since a zero-coupon bond has no profit, the collared stock position has the same profit as the bull spread.

Since the position consists of a long put and a short call, it is sometimes possible to construct what is known as a *zero-cost collar* by selecting K and K' so that $\mathcal{P}(K, T) = \mathcal{C}(K', T)$. The synthetic forward contract is an example of a zero-cost collar, but there are more interesting possibilities.

We show the payoff of the collar $\mathcal{P}(K, T) - \mathcal{C}(K, T)$ and the collared stock in figure 9.

Straddle

The *straddle* is position to use when we are expect that there is going to be a dramatic change in underlying values, but when we are not sure in which direction the price will change. The straddle is constructed with $\mathcal{P}(K, T) + \mathcal{C}(K, T)$. Its payoff is $|S_T - K|$ and its profit is $|S_T - K| - \mathcal{P}(K, T) - \mathcal{C}(K, T)$.

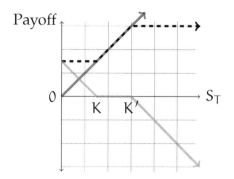

Figure 9: The collar, in light gray, has a payoff similar to a short forward contract. The flat spot between K and K', is a region where we do not have to sell. The collared stock position, in dark gray, is useful for hedging future sales of the underlying.

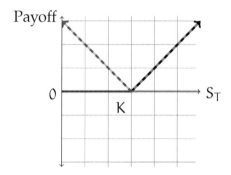

Figure 10: The straddle pays off when there is volatility in the underlying price. For a lower cost alternative, consider the strangle.

The opposite position, a *written straddle*, is $-(\mathcal{P}(K,T) + \mathcal{C}(K,T))$, and has payoff $-|S_T - K|$. Of course, by writing a straddle, we earn $\mathcal{P}(K, T) + \mathcal{C}(K, T)$, but risk that either one of them will be exercised.

Strangle

The *strangle* is used in similar circumstances to the straddle. The position is defined by

$$\mathcal{P}(K, T) + \mathcal{C}(K', T),$$

and has the payoff function

$$\begin{cases} K - S_T & \text{if } S_T < K, \\ 0 & \text{if } K \le S_T \le K', \\ S_T - K' & \text{if } K' < S_T. \end{cases}$$

Butterfly Spread

The butterfly spread is designed to profit from low volatility. The position consists of

$$\mathcal{C}(J, T) - 2\mathcal{C}(K, T) + \mathcal{C}(L, T),$$

where $J < K < L$. For the special case when $K - J = L - K$ – that is, when the exercise prices are evenly spaced – the payoff function for the butterfly spread is

$$\begin{cases} S_T - J, & \text{if } J \le S_T \le K \\ L - S_T, & \text{if } K \le S_T \le L \\ 0, & \text{otherwise.} \end{cases}$$

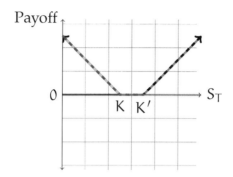

Figure 11: The strangle pays off when there is volatility in the underlying price. The strangle requires a larger price change than a straddle to achieve a positive payoff, but it costs less.

The long butterfly spread can be compared to the short straddle. Both reach their maximum payoff, and profit, at the underlying price K. The short straddle, however, can have unlimited losses. The butterfly spread cannot, but costs more to construct.

4.4.4 *Exercises*

14° Suppose that the American call A, Bermudan call B, and European call C, all have the same underlying, expiration date, and exercise price. Order the options by price, from least to greatest.

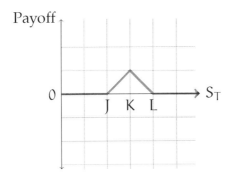

Figure 12: The long butterfly spread reaches its maximum payoff and profit when $S_T = K$.

15° The distribution of prices for S_T at time T is

$$S_T = \begin{cases} 80, & \text{with } p = 0.3 \\ 100, & \text{with } p = 0.5 \\ 120, & \text{with } p = 0.2 \end{cases}$$

Suppose you own the underlying and buy $\mathcal{P}(90, T)$. What is the standard deviation of the distribution of payoffs?

16° Find $\mathcal{P}(45, 0.25)$ if $\mathcal{C}(45, 0.25) = 2.9$, $S_0 = 42.25$, and $r = 0.044$.

17° Find S_0 if $\mathcal{C}(1100, 0.5) = 72.58$, $\mathcal{P}(1100, 0.5) = 100.50$, and $r = 0.035$.

18° Find T if $\mathcal{C}(100, T) = 6.91$, $\mathcal{P}(100, T) = 14.65$. and $S_0 = 89.55$.

19° Find $\mathcal{C}(11000, 1)$ if $\mathcal{P}(11000, 1) = 241.09$, $S_0 = 10151$, and $r = 0.077$.

20° Find K if $\mathcal{C}(K, 0.25) = 5.68$, $\mathcal{P}(K, 0.25) = 1.29$, $S_0 = 78.34$, and $r = 0.0565$.

21° Find r if $\mathcal{C}(650, 1) = 56.11$, $\mathcal{P}(650, 1) = 91.25$, and $S_0 = 676.78$.

22° Construct a straddle with a floor, a bond, and a put.

23° Construct a bull spread using put options.

24° Construct a bull spread using a bear spread and a bond.

25° A large construction project will need $20,000$ tons of steel in 6 months. The project manager is concerned about the price of steel. The price is currently 250 per ton, and the risk-free rate is 8%. The manager enters into forward contracts to buy 10000 tons. The manager also buys 5 call options, priced at 11000 each, to buy 5000 tons of steel at 375. What is her average cost per ton if the price rises to 400?

4.5 SOLUTIONS

1° By taking ownership of the annuity in a year, you become entitled to the remaining payments. The price of the annuity one year from now is the present value of the remaining payments then. We can compute this as $\ddot{a}_{\overline{3}|j}$, where $j = \frac{i^{(4)}}{4}$. The numerical answer is 111.15.

2° Note that $S_0 = 6.9 \times 5000$, and that $F_{0,T} = S_0 e^{rT} = 35197$.

3° Recall that $F_{0,1} = S_0 e^r$, so that $1100 = 1033 e^r$, and

$$r = \log\left(\frac{1100}{1033}\right).$$

4° The company is contracted to sell 5 kilograms at $S_0 e^{rT} = 679575$ each, for a profit of 39575 per kilogram. The company also sells 5 kilograms for 630000, for a loss of 10000 each. The total profit is $(5 \times 39575) + (5 \times (-10000)) = 147877$.

5° We will use the relation

$$P = (1-h)(S_T - C) + h(F_{0,T} - C),$$

where C represents the per unit cost of production. We must find the per unit forward price in order to use this relation – $F_{0,T} = S_0 e^{rT} = 0.42848$. We now solve for h in the relation.

$$h = \frac{P + C - S_T}{F_{0,T} - S_T}$$

so that $h = 0.7499$ and $1 - h = 0.25$.

6° We see that the average cost of natural gas was

$$\frac{1}{2}F_{0,T} + \frac{1}{2}S_T = 1864.$$

We also see that the profit earned by the forward contract was

$$S_T - F_{0,T} = S_T - S_0 e^{\frac{r}{2}} = 118,$$

so that

$$S_T = 118 + 1778 e^{\frac{r}{2}}.$$

Substitute this expression for S_T into the first equation and solve for $r = 0.03$.

A minor shortcut can be realized by noticing that the two set-up equations form a system of linear equations. We can almost immediately solve for $S_T = 1923$ and then solve for r in $1923 = 118 + 1778 e^{\frac{r}{2}}$.

7° We see that there are price declines as well as increases. It is possible that Ian faced a margin call, so we must reconstruct his margin account history from the closing prices. We do this by filling out the table

Day	Close	Balance	Deposit
1	760	310	350
2	510	60	
3	520	360	290
4	360	200	
5	600	590	150
6	800	790	
7	1000	990	

We note that the balance column contains Ian's margin balance after that day's settlement, and that margin deposits occur the morning after daily settlement. Notice that a margin call occurred when his balance hit the maintenance margin requirement, so that Ian was required to deposit 150 on the fifth morning. By adding up the deposits, we see that Ian deposited a total of 790. He earned a total of 200 margin, since he entered the position at 800 and closed it at 1000. The ratio is $r = 0.24$.

8° Use the interest rate swap formula to calculate $r = 2.98\%$.

9° Use the interest rate swap rate formula to calculate $r = 6.26\%$.

10° Use the interest rate swap formula to calculate $r = 3.79\%$.

11° Use the spot rates to calculate the forward rates. Use the interest rate swap formula to calculate $r = 10.3\%$.

12° Use the forward rates to calculate the spot rates. Use the interest rate swap formula to calculate $r = 15.0\%$.

13° We begin by calculating the fixed payment, using the interest rate swap pricing formula.

$$r = \frac{1 - v_3^3}{v_1^1 + v_2^2 + v_3^3} = 12.35\%.$$

This means that Macaulayco makes a series of payments $0.005B_0$, $-0.0025B_0$, and $-0.0185B_0$. The present value of the payments is

$$B_0 \left(\frac{0.005}{1.124} - \frac{0.0025}{1.126^2} - \frac{0.0185}{1.142^3} \right) = 1863.76,$$

so that $B_0 = 98917$.

14° The European call C can only be exercised on the expiration date. The Bermudan option B can be exercised on the expiration, and on a few other selected dates. The American option A can be exercised on any date before expiration. Because there is value in choice, we see that $C < B < A$.

15° The combination of the underlying and a long put is a floor on the total value. In particular, the payoff for the combination is a random variable P with distribution

$$P = \begin{cases} 90, & \text{with } p = 0.3 \\ 100, & \text{with } p = 0.5 \\ 120, & \text{with } p = 0.2 \end{cases}$$

We can readily compute the standard deviation as 10.44 by evaluating the formula $\sqrt{E[P^2] - E[P]^2}$.

16° Use put-call parity to solve for $\mathcal{P}(45, 0.25) = 4.16$.

17° $S_0 = 1053$

18° $T = 0.25$.

19° $\mathcal{C}(11000, 1) = 274.88$.

20° $K = 75$.

21° $r = 0.091$

22° $\text{Floor}(K) - K \cdot Z_{0,T} + \mathcal{P}(K, T)$

23° $\mathcal{P}(K', T) - \mathcal{P}(K, T)$

24° $K \cdot Z_{0,T} - \text{Bear}(K, K')$

25° We see that half of her steel will cost $S_0 e^{rT} = 350e^{0.04} = 364.284$. A quarter of her steel will cost $S_T = 400$. The project manager spent 55000 to buy call options on 5000 tons of steel. The total cost for those 5000 tons, including the option premium is $(375 \times 5000) + 55000e^{0.04} = 1932245$, so that the average cost per ton is 386.45. Putting these costs together, we see that her average cost is 378.75.

5

ASSET-LIABILITY MANAGEMENT

A firm with outstanding liabilities will want to pay them on time and at the lowest possible cost. As with any plan, risks can frustrate the liability payment schedule. Risks include the possibility of funds being scheduled to be disbursed too soon or too late to pay a liability. If the funds are disbursed too soon, the firm faces the cost of lost interest – that is, the funds could have been earning interest until the liability was due, but were not because the funds were disbursed too soon. If the funds are disbursed too late, the firm will have to seek other forms of financing, with all of their associated costs.

Interest rate risk is another major risk. A firm might use a portfolio of bonds to pay for its regularly scheduled liabilities, and their value is obviously tied to the prevailing interest rate.

In this chapter, we will examine the planning methods used to control these risks.

5.1   DURATION

Our goal is to find a measure of interest rate sensitivity. We claim that the length of time over which the cash flows occur is a natural measure of price risk. This could be intuitively obvious. A small interest rate change will not have a large effect on the present value of near-term cash flows, but the small change will compound over many periods.

Consider a sequence of cash flows $\{c_t\}$ and let $P(i)$ denote its present value, as a function of i. We define the *duration* of the cash flow as the quantity

$$D = \frac{\sum_t tc_t v^t}{P(i)}.$$

By grouping the terms, we can think of the duration of a weighted average of the *times* when a cash flow occurs, weighted by the present values of the cash flow. We can also define the *modified duration* as the quantity

$$DM = vD = \frac{\sum_t tc_t v^{t+1}}{P(i)}.$$

Notice that the modified duration's numerator is the minus derivative of the present value of the cash flows. In particular, each term of the sum is in the form

$$tc_t v^{t+1} = \frac{tc_t}{(1+i)^{t+1}} = -\frac{d}{di}\frac{c_t}{(1+i)^t}.$$

In fact, we can define the modified duration by

$$DM = -\frac{P'(i)}{P(i)}.$$

The modified duration lets us calculate the duration for sequences of cash flows that are intractable from the basic definition of the duration. For example, if C is a sequence of cash flows, $D_{vC} = D_v + 1$. In words, deferring a sequence of cash flows increases the sequence's duration by 1. The proof is simple and instructive, and is left as an exercise.

With knowledge of the duration or modified duration and the current price, we can construct *linear approximations* of the price curve near an interest rate i. This is standard calculus, using slightly different notation. In particular, we can write the approximate change in price (ΔP) in response to the change (Δi) as

$$\Delta P \approx -(DM)P(i)(\Delta i).$$

We can construct second-order approximations using the price function's convexity, which we define as

$$Conv = \frac{P''(i)}{P(i)}.$$

The convexity is just a scaled version of the second derivative of the price function. We can approximate changes in the price function as

$$\Delta P \approx -(DM)P(i)(\Delta i) + (Conv)P(i)(\Delta i)^2.$$

This formula is effectively an application of Taylor's theorem in disguise.

We can use the duration method to approximate a portfolio's response of a change in prevailing interest rates, as well. Of course, we can compute the duration of the portfolio directly, using the definition of the duration. And we will begin there, to derive a useful result. Let A and B be different assets, and let a_t and b_t be cash flows generated by A and B respectively. As usual, we use the convention that A and B denote the present value of the assets, as well. We can calculate the duration of the combined asset $A + B$ as

$$D_{A+B} = \frac{\sum_t t(a_t + b_t)v^t}{A + B}$$

$$= \frac{\sum_t ta_t v^t + tb_t v^t}{A + B}$$

$$= \frac{\left[\sum_t ta_t v^t\right] + \left[\sum_t tb_t v^t\right]}{A + B}$$

$$= \frac{AD_A + BD_B}{A + B},$$

where D_A and D_B are the durations of A and B, respectively. This means that the duration of the combination of assets $A + B$ is the weighted average of the durations, weighted by the present values A and B. By induction, this result generalizes to any number of assets. This fact is very useful for theoretical and problem solving reasons. In particular, it can greatly simplify the calculation of the duration of assets with varying cash flows. Also, some exam problems give us the durations and present values of assets in a portfolio, and ask us to calculate the duration of the portfolio. These problems do not typically give us enough information to solve the problem directly from the definition.

We will now calculate the duration of an n year bond with yearly coupon payments. We recall that a basic bond can be constructed as an annuity immediate that pays Fr, and a cash flow of C at the end of n years. Indeed, the basic price formula for bonds tells us that the price of a bond is

$$(Fr)a_{\overline{n}|} + Cv^n.$$

We can see that the duration of the cash flow C at the end of n years is

$$D_C = \frac{nCv^n}{Cv^n} = n.$$

We will state without proof that the duration of an annuity immediate is

$$D_{a_{\overline{n}|}} = \frac{(Ia)_{\overline{n}|}}{a_{\overline{n}|}},$$

and leave the proof as an exercise. In any event, we can use the combination formula to find the duration for the bond

$$D_B = \frac{Fr(Ia)_{\overline{n}|} + nCv^n}{Fra_{\overline{n}|} + Cv^n}.$$

Even some perpetuities have a finite duration. Intuitively, this means that the perpetuity's present value is concentrated in the first 'few' payments. In other words, the sequence of present values of cash flows converges to 0 quickly enough that the series

$$\sum_{t=1}^{\infty} tc_t v^t$$

converges.

5.2 IMMUNIZATION

In order for a firm to pay its liabilities, it must have enough money to do so. But the firm must not set aside too much, since it could be used more productively as capital. Symbolically, we say that

$$\sum_t A_t v^t = \sum_t L_t v^t,$$

where A_t is a cash flow generated by an asset at time t and L_t is a payment made to service a liability at time t. We call this *present value matching*.

Define a function $M(i)$ by

$$M(i) = \left[\sum_t \frac{A_t}{(1+i)^t} \right] - \left[\sum_t \frac{L_t}{(1+i)^t} \right].$$

This function represents the difference between the present values of the assets and liabilities, as a function of the interest rate. Of course, we want this value to be 0. But we also want it to be a minimum at the initial rate of interest, so that interest rate changes leave us in a position where we can still pay all the liabilities. If $M'(i) = 0$, then

$$\frac{d}{di} \sum_t A_t v^t = \frac{d}{di} \sum_t L_t v^t.$$

In particular, their durations match. We have discussed duration as a measure of an asset's sensitivity to interest rate changes. A liability, being a 'negative asset', also responds to interest rate changes, and those changes can be measured using duration and convexity. Having arranged asset-liability matching, we would like for the assets to have the same duration as the liabilities. Any other arrangement would expose the firm to interest rate risk. If the liabilities are more sensitive to interest rate changes than the assets, then a decrease in interest rates can cause the present value of the liabilities to increase beyond the present value of the assets. If the assets are more responsive to interest rate changes, an increase in interest rates can cause the present value of the assets to decreaase below the present value of the liabilities. If the durations are equal, then the prices of the assets and liabilities both shift by equal amounts in response to an interest rate change.

If a portfolio has satisfies this condition, together with present value matching, then we have achieved *duration matching*. Because the present values are equal, the durating matching condition implies that $D_A = D_L$. Note that $D_A =$

D_L does not necessarily imply that the present values of the assets and liabilities are equal.

Since we have assumed that $M(i)$ is a local minimum, we see that $M''(i) > 0$. This means that

$$\frac{d^2}{di^2} \sum_t A_t v^t > \frac{d^2}{di^2} \sum_t L_t v^t.$$

We can see that this means that the assets have greater convexity than the liabilities. Since the duration is a function of i, it responds to changes in i. Intuitively, the condition means that the assets' duration is more sensitive to interest rate changes, and always in the *right direction*. The assets duration will decrease less than the liabilities', in the case that interest rates fall. And the assets' duration will increase more than the liabilities', if the interest rates fall. Now, even if there is an interest rate change with consequent changes on asset and liability values and duration, we are still in a position to pay the liabilities and still protected from interest rate risk.

A portfolio is said to be *immunized* if M is at a local minimum at i, the current interest rate. The portfolio is *fully immunized* if M is at a minimum at i, and it is a global minimum. In particular, if a portfolio is fully immunized, then it will always be able to pay its liabilities, in spite of *any* interest rate change.

5.3 EXERCISES

1° Calculate the duration of a unit annuity immediate.

2° Calculate the duration of a unit annuity due.

3° Calculate the duration of the unit perpetuity immediate.

4° A portfolio contains two bonds. The first is worth 970, and a duration of 5.2. The second is worth 560 and has a duration of 15. What is the portfolio's duration?

5° A portfolio contains two bonds. The first is worth 990, and a duration of 1.375. The second is worth 985 and has a duration of 10.11. What is the portfolio's duration?

6° A portfolio contains 3 zero coupon bonds, each of which has a face value of 1000. One is redeemable in a year, another in 5, and the last in 15. If the prevailing interest rate is 6.8%, what is the portfolio's duration?

7° A portfolio contains

- 3 bonds worth 980 each, with durations of 2.125;

- 5 bonds worth 4700 each, with durations of 6.175.

What is the portfolio's duration?

8° A portfolio contains

- One 20 year, 10000 par value bond with coupon rate $r^{(2)} = 6\%$.

- Ten 10 year, 1000 par value bonds with coupon rate $r^{(2)} = 7\%$.

If the prevailing interest rate is $i^{(2)} = 5\%$, what is the portfolio's duration?

9° When the prevailing interest rate was $i = 5.75\%$, a bond cost 951.48 and had a duration of 24.61. What is the approximate price if interest rates changed to 6%?

10° When the prevailing interest rate was $i = 4.38\%$, a bond cost 984.33 and had a duration of 9.38. How large was the interest rate change if the price changed to 948.95?

11° A portfolio contains two bonds. One is worth 950 and has a duration of 12.75. The other is worth 1200 and has a duration of 35.1. Both are priced to yield 6.5%. By how much does the portfolio change in value if interest rates change to 6.7%?

12° Show that deferring a sequence of cash flows by k periods increases the cash flow's duration by k.

13° Find the duration of a geometric annuity.

14° A company has a liability for 3000 due in 1 year, and a liability for 5000 due in 2 years. The company has the following investments to choose from:

- A zero-coupon bond with face value of 1000, earning a yearly effective rate of 3.25%, redeemable in a year;

- A zero-coupon bond with face value of 1000, earning a yearly effective rate of 3.5%, redeemable in two years.

What is the total cost of paying the liabilities?

15° A company has a liability for 5000 due in 6 months, a liability for 10000 due in 1 year, and a liability for 50000 due in 5 years. The company has the following investments to choose from:

- A zero-coupon bond with face value of 1000, earning a yearly effective rate of 3%, redeemable in six months;

- A zero-coupon bond with face value of 1000, earning a yearly effective rate of 4%, redeemable in one year;

- A zero-coupon bond with face value of 2500, earning a yearly effective rate of 6%, redeemable in five years.

What is the total cost of paying the liabilities?

16° A company has a liability for 3000 due in 1 year, and a liability for 5000 due in 2 years. The company has the following investments to choose from:

B_1 A 3% yearly coupon bond with face value of 1000, earning a yearly effective rate of 3.25%, redeemable in a year;

B_2 A 3% yearly coupon bond with face value of 1000, earning a yearly effective rate of 3.5%, redeemable in two years.

What is the total cost of paying the liabilities?

17° A company has a liability for 2000 due in 1 year, and a liability for 3000 due in 5 years. The company has the following investments to choose from:

B$_1$ A 4% yearly coupon bond with face value of 500, earning a yearly effective rate of 5%, redeemable in a year;

B$_2$ A 3.5% yearly coupon bond with face value of 10000, earning a yearly effective rate of 5.25%, redeemable in five years.

What is the total cost of paying the liabilities?

18° A company has a single liability of 15000 due in 3 years. The company has the following investments to choose from.

B$_1$ A 1000 par value, one year zero coupon bond earning 4%.

B$_{10}$ A 1000 par value, 10 year zero coupon bond earning 4%.

How many units of each should the company buy to duration match their liability?

19° A company has a single liability of 50000 due in 4 years. The company has the following investments to choose from.

B$_2$ A 1000 par value, 2 year zero coupon bond earning 5%.

B$_5$ A 1000 par value, 5 year zero coupon bond earning 5%.

How many units of each should the company buy to duration match their liability?

5.4 SOLUTIONS

1° Recall that the unit annuity immediate has unit payments at the end of n periods. We write

$$D = \frac{\sum_{k=1}^{n} kv^k}{a_{\overline{n}|}} = \frac{(Ia)_{\overline{n}|}}{a_{\overline{n}|}}.$$

2° Recall that the unit annuity immediate has unit payments at the beginning of n periods. We write

$$D = \frac{\sum_{k=0}^{n-1} kv^k}{\ddot{a}_{\overline{n}|}} = \frac{\sum_{k=1}^{n-1} kv^k}{\ddot{a}_{\overline{n}|}} = \frac{(Ia)_{\overline{n-1}|}}{\ddot{a}_{\overline{n}|}}.$$

3° Recall that the present value of the unit perpetuity immediate is

$$a_{\overline{\infty}|} = \frac{1}{i}.$$

We will calculate the duration by way of calculating the
modified duration.

$$DM = \frac{P'(i)}{P(i)} = -\frac{-\frac{1}{i^2}}{\frac{1}{i}} = -\frac{1}{i}.$$

Since $DM = vD$, we see that

$$D = -\kappa\frac{1}{i} = -\frac{1}{d}.$$

4° We calculate

$$D_P = \frac{(970 \times 5.2) + (560 \times 15)}{970 + 560} = 8.79.$$

5° We calculate

$$D_P = \frac{(990 \times 1.375) + (985 \times 10.11)}{990 + 985} = 5.73.$$

6° The duration for a zero coupon bond is just the time until the bond is redeemable.

We calculate the portfolio's duration as

$$D_P = \frac{1000(v + 5v^5 + 15v^{15})}{1000(v + v^5 + v^{15})} = 4.99.$$

7° We calculate the duration as

$$D = \frac{(3 \times 980 \times 2.125) + (5 \times 4700 \times 6.175)}{(3 \times 980) + (5 \times 4700)} = 5.73.$$

8° We calculate the durations as

$$D_1 = \frac{30(Ia)_{\overline{40|}} + 40 \cdot 1000 \cdot v^{40}}{30a_{\overline{40|}} + 1000v^{40}} = 14.391$$

and

$$D_2 = \frac{35(Ia)_{\overline{20}|} + 20 \cdot 1000 \cdot v^{20}}{35a_{\overline{40}|} + 1000v^{20}} = 15.130.$$

In the course of calculating the durations, we calculated the prices for each bond, which we circled in our scratch work. Let P_1 and P_2 be the prices. Then the portfolio duration is

$$D_P = \frac{(D_1 \times P_1) + (10 \times D_2 \times P_2)}{P_1 + P_2}$$

$$= 14.77.$$

9° We begin by converting the duration to a modified duration $DM = vD = 24.61$. We see that the interest rates change by $\Delta i = 0.25\%$. Then the approximate price change is

$$\Delta P \approx -(DM)P(i)(\Delta i) = -55.36.$$

We calculate the new price as approximately 896.12.

10° We begin by converting the duration to a modified duration $DM = vD = 8.986$. We see the approximate price change is

$$984.33 - 948.95 = 35.38 = \Delta P \approx -(DM)P(i)(\Delta i),$$

so that

$$\Delta i \approx -\frac{\Delta P}{(DM)P(i)} = 0.4\%.$$

11° We calculate the duration of the portfolio as

$$D_P = \frac{(950 \times 12.75) + (1200 \times 35.1)}{950 + 1200} = 25.22442,$$

so that $DM = 23.6948$. We use the price change formula to calculate

$$\Delta P = -DM \cdot P(i)(\Delta i) = -101.85$$

12° Let C be a sequence of cash flows, and let $P_C(i)$ be its present value. Similarly, let $P_{vC}(i)$ be the present value of vC. We calculate

$$DM_{vC} = -\frac{P'_{vC}(i)}{P_{vC}} = -\frac{1}{vP_C(i)} \cdot \frac{d}{di}\left(\frac{1}{1+i}P_C(i)\right)$$
$$= -\frac{1}{vP_C(i)}\left(vP'_C(i) - P_C(i)v^2\right) = DM_C + v.$$

We apply the definition of the modified duration to find that

$$D_{vC} = \kappa(DM_C + v) = D_C + 1.$$

13° The formula is

$$D = \frac{n(rv)^n}{1 - (rv)^n} + \frac{\kappa}{\kappa - r}.$$

The formula can be found by taking the derivative of the present value of the geometric annuity, and dividing it by the present value. The result is the modified duration of the geometric annuity. The duration is found by fast-forwarding the modified duration. *We suggest memorizing this formula.* The derivation is somewhat time consuming and error prone.

14° We write the equation of value

$$3 \times 1000v_{3.25\%} + 5 \times 1000v_{3.5\%} = 7573.12.$$

15° We write the equation of value

$$5 \times 1000v_{3\%}^{\frac{1}{2}} + 10 \times 1000v_{4\%} + 20 \times 2500v_{6\%}^{5} = 50904.94.$$

16° We write the equation of value

$$P = x_1 P_1 + x_2 P_2,$$

where x_k is the number of k year bonds necessary, and P_k is the price of a k year bond. We begin by calculating x_2. We see that the company must pay 5000 in two years. A unit of B_2 will pay 1030 in two years, so that

$$x_2 = \frac{5000}{1030} = 4.854.$$

Similarly, A unit of B_1 will pay 1030 in one year. But a unit of B_2 will pay 30 in a year. We see that

$$x_1 = \frac{3000 - 30x_2}{1030} = 2.771.$$

We price these bonds using the usual techniques, so that

$$P_1 = 997.58$$
$$P_2 = 990.50$$

and

$$P = x_1 P_1 + x_2 P_2 = 7572.78.$$

17° We write the equation of value

$$P = x_1 P_1 + x_2 P_2,$$

where x_k is the number of k year bonds necessary, and P_k is the price of a k year bond. We begin by calculating x_2.

$$x_2 = \frac{3000}{10350} = 0.2899.$$

Similarly, A unit of B_1 will pay 520 in one year. But a unit of B_2 will pay 350 in a year. We see that

$$x_1 = \frac{2000 - 350x_2}{520} = 3.797.$$

We price these bonds using the usual techniques, so that

$$P_1 = 495.24$$
$$P_2 = 9247.55$$

and

$$P = x_1 P_1 + x_2 P_2 = 4560.93.$$

18° If the assets and liabilities are present value matched,

$$15000v^3 = B_1 v + B_{10} v^{10}.$$

If the assets and liabilites are duration matched as well,

$$3 \times 15000v^3 = B_1v + 10B_{10}v^{10}.$$

The task is to solve these equations for B_1 and B_{10}. We see immediately that

$$B_1v = 15000v^3 - B_{10}v^{10} = 3 \times 15000v^3 - 10B_{10}v^{10}.$$

We solve for $B_{10} = 4386.44$, and substitute in to find that $B_1 = 10786.49$. Finally, we see we need 4.386 units of B_2 and 10.786 units of B_1.

19° If the assets and liabilities are present value matched,

$$50000v^4 = B_2v^2 + B_5v^5.$$

If the assets and liabilites are duration matched as well,

$$4 \times 50000v^4 = 2B_2v^2 + 5B_5v^5.$$

The task is to solve these equations for $B_2 = 15117.16$ and $B_5 = 35000$. Finally, we see we need 15.117 units of B_1 and 35 units of B_2.

6

1° At the beginning of the year, a portfolio contained

- 1400 worth of stock, which earns dividends continuously at a rate $\delta = 0.0392$,

- a 5 year zero coupon 1000 par bond, priced to yield an effective rate of $i = 6\%$, and expiring on July 1.

There was a contribution of 300 on April 1 and a withdrawal of 400 on November 15. All contributions and interest earned are invested in fractional shares of stock. All withdrawls are funded by selling fractional shares of stock. Assuming continuous compounding, what is the time weighted yield for the portfolio?

A. 4.0%   B. 4.4%   C. 5.6%   D. 7.1%   E. 9.0%

2° Ashley bought the combination $P(100, 0.5) + C(100, 0.5) + S$ at time $t = 0$. He bought the underlying at 110. His profit at time T is 18.21 per unit of the combination. Terri

177

bought the combination $\mathcal{C}(100,0.5) + S$ at time $t = 0$ and made a profit of 26.91. Hogarth entered into the position $3(\mathcal{C}(100,0.5) - \mathcal{P}(100,0.5))$ at time $t = 0$. If $S_0 = 110$ and $r = 0.085$, what is Hogarth's profit?

A. 53.41 B. 61.20 C. 69.00 D. 76.63 E. 132.58

$3°$ A heavy industry firm enters into a forward contract to sell a fusion locomotive for 25 million, for delivery in 5 years. To finance the project, the firm enters into a loan that costs a yearly effective rate of 4%, and uses the proceeds to buy a five year annuity due that pays 3.5 million every year and earns the risk-free rate, 3.5%. The firm pays loan interest every year, and pays off the loan balance at the end of five years. What is the firm's profit?

A. 4.69 B. 4.86 C. 5.14 D. 5.37 E. 5.88

$4°$ Janice enters into a 20 year mortgage for $200,000$. The mortgage a yearly effective rate of 4.5%. Janice pays $20,000$ a year, for the first 10 years. How much interest does she pay in the 15th payment?

A. 807 B. 1409 C. 1902 D. 6292 E. 7772

$5°$ An account earns interest at a force of

$$\delta(t) = \frac{2\alpha t}{1 + \alpha t^2}.$$

An initial deposit of 100 accumulates to 260 in 12 years. A deposit of 50 is made after 15 years. How much is in the account after 20 years?

A. 448 B. 452 C. 467 D. 622 E. 772

6° A portfolio contains a level payment annuity paying 100 per month for 10 years, and three 30 year 1000 face value bonds paying a coupon rate of 6% convertible semiannually. If the prevailing effective interest rate is $i = 7.5\%$, what is the portfolio's duration?

A. 4.44 B. 6.11 C. 6.36 D. 12.9 E. 14.8

7° Stable Heritage, LTD, issues monthly dividends. The last dividend was for 50 cents, and each dividend is 0.25% larger than the previous one. Luther enters into a forward contract to receive ownership of 100 shares in 6 months, after the 6th dividend is disbursed. Payment will occur in three months. What is the prepaid forward price if the risk-free rate 7.0%?

A. 8542 B. 10809 C. 13352 D. 15743 E. 15861

8° A one year call option on S, with an exercise price of 100, costs 4.63, and one year put option on S, with the same exercise price, costs 9.59. The price S_0 is 88.93. What is the duration of a one year, 1000 par value bond issuing monthly coupons for 20?

A. 0.78 B. 0.82 C. 0.88 D. 0.91 E. 1.16

9° A 5 year bond has a coupon rate of 8.5%, and a face value of 1000. The bond is priced using the spot rates

n	s_n
1	6.7%
2	6.3%
3	6.0%
4	5.9%
5	5.85%

How much of the principal is paid in the third coupon?

A. 12 B. 37 C. 52 D. 63 E. 67

10° A perpetuity due begins paying 100, and the payment increases by 6% each month for 4 years. The payments then remain level for 10 years. The payments then decrease by 2% per month. If the perpetuity earns a nominal rate of 6.5%, convertible quarterly, what is the accumulated value after 15 years?

A. 173197 B. 190255 C. 398654 D. 455591 E. 799725

11° Irene purchases an annuity whose payments start at 100 and increase by 6% each payment for 9 payments. The payments then remain constant for 20 payments. The annuity earns at 6%. After the 8th payment, Irene sells the annuity an purchases a 30 year level payment annuity at the same interest rate. What is her new level payment?

A. 134.47 B. 139.48 C. 143.74 D. 147.14 E. 153.11

12° Each year, for 5 years, Karen buys a 5 year 1000 face value bond paying a yearly coupon of 100. What is the total interest paid by the bonds in the 4th year, if all the bonds yield 8%?

A. 18.66 B. 61.34 C. 93.32 D. 306.68 E. 344.74

13° Waldo's retirement annuity earns 8% and pays 10000 a year for 10 years and 15000 a year for 5 years. Waldo spends 10000 in the first year after he retires, and 7000 every year after that. He deposits the remainder in a savings account earning 3%. Waldo hopes his savings last another 15 years after the annuity ends. How much larger would his yearly payment be if he bought a 15 year level payment annuity earning 7% instead of making 15 level withdrawals from his savings?

A. 398 B. 720 C. 1123 D. 1756 E. 2025

14° A call option expiring at time $T = 0.25$, with exercise price $K = 65$ costs 13.28615. The underlying currently costs $S_0 = 76.882$. A straddle centered at 85 costs 10.52119. A butterfly spread with strike prices $65 - 75 - 85$ costs 3.42027. If $S_T = 80$, what is the profit for $\mathcal{P}(75, T) - \mathcal{P}(80, T)$?

A. 0.926 B. 1.948 C. 3.402 D. 5.855 E. 6.185

15° A loan for $30,000$ at $i = 9\%$ will be paid for using the coupons from a $100,000$ par value bond. The bond is priced to yield $j = 4.5\%$ and costs 108144.14. The loan balance at the end of the third year is 22460.37. What is the bond worth immediately after the last loan payment?

A. 96832 B. 102576 C. 106702 D. 109441 E. 110440

16° Henrietta purchases a 30 year 7.5% coupon rate bond immediately after the 5th coupon payment. The bond is priced to 5.4% if held to maturity. Henrietta invests the coupon payments in a mutual fund earning $j = 13.5\%$. This investment position accumulates 2983.53 for Henrietta. What was the true yield rate for the bond?

A. 3.0% B. 4.4% C. 6.3% D. 6.4% E. 10.6%

17° Simon makes monthly payments into a continously compounding retirement account starting on his 30th birthday. Simon beigns making yearly withdrawals of 8000, starting on his 65th birthday, for 25 years. If the account earns a yearly effective rate of 6.5%, what is his monthly payment?

A. 63.69 B. 67.47 C. 70.05 D. 76.85 E. 85.25

18° Denise pays 1109.53 per month for a 15 year loan that charges a nominal rate of 4%. How many points was she charged if her effective yearly rate is 6.5%?

A. 9.75 B. 10.5 C. 12.0 D. 14.1 E. 16.7

19° Franz buys a 20000 par value bond with a yearly 5% coupon, priced to yield 8%. He deposits the coupons into an account earning 10%. He withdraws the interest earned in that account and deposits it into an account earning 12%. What was Franz' effective yield?

A. 7.5% B. 7.9% C. 8.2% D. 8.8% E. 9.7%

20° Johan deposits 500 into an account that earns an effective yearly rate i. The amount in Johans account after 24 years is 7 times the amount in his account after 8 years. Nina deposits 10 into an account every month. Her account balance is the same as Johan's after 9 years. How much will Nina have after 20 years?

A. 2754 B. 5169 C. 5693 D. 6008 E. 6567

21° A company must pay liabilities of 1000 in 6 months and 3000 in one year. To fund the liabilities, the company can purchase:

- A 6 month zero coupon bond yielding a nominal yearly rate of 6%,

- A one year bond, with a nominal coupon rate of 8%.

If the total cost to match the liabilities exactly is 3784.71, what is the nominal yield for the one year bond?

A. 4.2% B. 4.7% C. 6.3% D. 6.5% E. 6.3%

22° Wilma owns three perpetuities. The first one pays P at the end of each year. The second one pays 2P at the end of every two years. The third one pays 4P at the end of every four years. She paid a total of $800,000$ for them. Laverne's perpetuity earns the same interest rate as Wilma's. It pays 10000 per year, and cost 360000. What is P?

A. 7544 B. 9384 C. 11423 D. 13677 E. 14346

23° Frederick buys a 1000 face value, 10 year bond with a redemption value of 1250, priced to yield a nominal rate of 7%, convertible semi-annually. Frederick paid 10% more than George, who bought a 1000 face value, 10 year bond with the same coupon and interest rates. How much interest did Frederick's bond pay during the 5th coupon?

A. 3.89 B. 9.39 C. 26.73 D. 37.43 E. 43.94

24° Claire buys a house with a 30-year $500000 mortgage with monthly payments. She is charged a nominal rate of 7.3% and 5.5 points. Claire pays 5000 a month, for the first 15 years. How much more interest would Claire have paid if she made level payments for 30 years?

A. 32000 B. 55000 C. 77000 D. 108000 E. 184000

25° Globex Corp. takes out a 10 year loan for 1000000. The loan costs a yearly effective rate of 8%. Each year, except the first, Globex makes interest payments. Each year, except the first and second, Globex makes deposits into a fund earning 11%. At the end of 10 years, Globex uses the fund to pay the loan balance. How much does Globex pay to service the loan, over its entire life?

A. 1429000 B. 1506000 C. 1728000 D. 1882000 E. 2931000

26° A perpetuity pays 100 in the first period, and pays 1 more each period after the first. The perpetuity cost 4444.44. Eric receives the first payment, and Eric and Kyle alternate thereafter. What is the present value of Eric's payments?

A. 1401 B. 1479 C. 2181 D. 2247 E. 2484

27° Gemma made 100 monthly payments of 300 each on a loan that charged a nominal rate of 15% interest. After the 100th payment, Gemma refinanced the loan. The new loan charges a nominal 9% and has 100 monthly payments of 75. What was her original principal?

A. 7107 B. 7537 C. 8026 D. 14080 E. 15551

28° InvesTrust Bank enters into a forward contract to purchase 500 bonds with par value 1000, paying a coupon rate of 6%, convertible semiannually, and currently priced to yield 4.8%, convertible semi-annually. The contract stipulates that delivery will occur in 1 year, and that payment is to occur now. What is the total amound paid?

A. 518260 B. 543435 C. 547212 D. 543794 E. 578240

29° An investment costs $P(i) = \frac{100}{i} + \frac{1}{i^2}$. If $i = 6\%$, what is its duration?

A. 20.2   B. 24.2   C. 27.1   D. 38.6   E. 44.1

30° A 10 year, 1000 par value bond with nominal coupon rate of 10%, convertible semiannually, yields a nominal 8%. Carter bought the bond when it was issued. The bond is currently worth 1093.85. How many years has Carter owned the bond?

A. 5   B. 6   C. 7   D. 10   E. 12

31° A portfolio contains bonds with value and duration

Value	Duration
0.5	4.7598
1.5	12.3859
2.5	25.987
3.5	31.3719

valued in millions. The current interest rate is 6.5%. How much would the portfolio's value change if interest rates changed to 6.75%?

A. −460000   B. −451000   C. −187000   D. 53000   E. 373000

32° A 30 year bond with 1000 par value and an 8% nominal coupon rate and a 5% nominal yield, both convertible quarterly, costs 15.4% more than an n year bond with otherwise identical terms. What is n?

A. 5   B. 7.5   C. 12   D. 15   E. 18

186

33° TAN Applied Bioscience enters into a 20 year loan for 500,000. The loan costs a nominal rate of 11.3% interest, convertible quarterly. TAN makes quarterly interest payments of I. TAN also makes quarterly payments of D into an investment fund earning 12%, for the purposes of paying the principal at the end of 20 years.

After 3 years, TAN refinances the loan, and secures a 5% nominal interest rate. TAN continues paying the loan interest I' each quarter, and deposits $D + I - I'$ into the fund. What is the fund balance after paying the loan?

A. 150000 B. 164000 C. 582000 D. 1360000 E. 1720000

34° Hyacinth makes monthly deposits of 100 into a risky investment account that earns a yearly nominal rate of 12% convertible monthly. Hyacinth also deposits 300 a month into an index fund that earns a yearly nominal rate of 8% convertible monthly. After 25 years, Hyacinth transfers all her money into a low risk bond fund earning a nominal 3% convertible monthly. For 30 years, she makes monthly withdrawals, starting at X, and increasing by 1% each month. What is X?

A. 1117 B. 1227 C. 1818 D. 1822 E. 2008

35° Egalite Insurance offers a 20 year geometric annuity. It earns 6%, and the payments decrease by 8% each year. What is the annuity's duration?

A. 5.41 B. 8.82 C. 27.17 D. 33.76 E. 55.89

SOLUTIONS

1° We must find the time weighted yield. We fill out the following table:

Date	Stock	Bond	Balance	Contribution
1/1	1400	971.29	2371.29	–
4/1	1413.79	985.54	2399.33	300
7/1	2730.67	0	–	–
11/15	2771.11	0	2771.11	–400
1/1	2382.75	0	2382.75	–

We will demonstrate how to fill out the table.

We are told that there is 1400 worth of stock in the account at the start of the year. We can find the amount of the bond in the account by discounting the par value for the time until it expires: $1000(1+i)^{-0.5} = 971.29$. The total balance at the start of the year is 2371.29.

There is a contribution on April 1, so we must find the balances again. We see that we have $1400e^{0.25\delta} = 1413.79$ worth of stock. We price the bond on 4/1 by discounting for 0.25 years: $1000(1+i)^{-0.25} = 985.54$. The total balance is 2399.33.

For 7/1, we find the balance for stock, noting that there was a contribution of 300 in the last period, and that the bond was redeemed and revinested, so that the stock column contains $(300 + 1413.79)e^{0.25\delta} + 1000$. We set the bond column to zero. We purposefully leave the balance column empty, because since there is no contribution on this date, we will not use the balance on this date to calculate the time weighted yield.

For 11/15, we see that it has been 4.5 months since the the bond was redeemed and reinvested in stock. So we must find the new stock balance by compounding for 4.5 months: $2730.67e^{0.375\delta} = 2771.11$. This is also the balance before contributions.

Finally, 1/1. We must find the stock balance and the total balance. The stock balance is $(2771.11 - 400)e^{0.125\delta} = 2382.75$. This is the total balance, as well.

We now have enough information to compute the time weighted yield. Recall that

$$(1+j) = \left(\frac{b_1}{b_0 + c_0}\right)\left(\frac{b_2}{b_1 + c_1}\right) \cdots \left(\frac{b_n}{b_{n-1} + c_{n-1}}\right)$$

We read off those values from the table, so that $1 + j = 1.0438$ and $j = 4.4\%$.

A. 4.0% **B. 4.4%** C. 5.6% D. 7.1% E. 9.0%

2° First, note that the position $\mathcal{P}(K,T) + \mathcal{C}(K,T)$ is a straddle, with payoff $|S_T - K|$. If we add the payoff for S at time T to the payoff for the straddle, we end up with the payoff

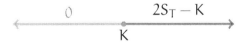

Since there is a positive profit, we know that $S_T > K$. We compare Ashley's profit to Terri's:

$$18.21 = 2S_T - K - S_0 e^{rT} - \mathcal{C}(K, T)e^{rT} - \mathcal{P}(K, T)e^{rT}$$
$$26.91 = 2S_T - K - S_0 e^{rT} - \mathcal{C}(K, T)e^{rT}$$

Subtracting Ashley's profit from Terri's, we find that $\mathcal{P}(K, T)e^{rT} = 8.7$, and that $\mathcal{P}(K, T) = 8.338$. We use put-call parity for time $t = 0$ to calculate $\mathcal{C}(K, T) = 22.499$. Then we solve for S_T in

$$26.91 = 2S_T - K - S_0 e^{rT} - \mathcal{C}(K, T)e^{rT},$$

so that

$$S_T = \frac{26.91 + K + S_0 e^{rT} + \mathcal{C}(K, T)e^{rT}}{2} = 132.58$$

Now, consider Hogarth's position,

$$3\left(\mathcal{C}(K, T) - \mathcal{P}(K, T)\right),$$

which we recognize as three synthetic forward contracts. The total payoff is $3(S_T - K)$, so that the profit is

$$3\left(S_T - K - \mathcal{C}(K, T)e^{rT} + \mathcal{P}(K, T)e^{rT}\right) = 53.41.$$

A. 53.41 B. 61.20 C. 69.00 D. 76.63 E. 132.58

3° We begin by calculating the present value of the annuity due, since this is the loan principal. We use the equation of value

$$B_0 = 3.5\ddot{a}_{\overline{5}|3.5\%} = 16.36$$

The firm pays 0.654 in interest each year. This means that, in present value terms, the firm pays $0.654s_{\overline{5}|3.5\%} = 3.5$ to service the interest. In addition, the firm pays 16.35 to pay the loan balance, for a total cost of 19.86. The total profit is 5.14.

A. 4.69 B. 4.86 **C. 5.14** D. 5.37 E. 5.88

4° We use the BAII Plus time value functions to calculate these figures.

Her balance after 10 years is 64829.70. For the purposes of problem solving, we can think of her as just starting a 10 year loan for 64829.70 at the same interest rate as before.

We calculate that her new monthly payments are 8193.10. We use the interest amortization formula to calculate

$$Int_k = P(1 - v^{n-k+1}) = P(1 - v^{10-5+1}) = 1901.65.$$

A. 807 B. 1409 **C. 1902** D. 6292 E. 7772

5° We begin by defining

$$r(t) = \int_0^t \frac{2\alpha t}{1 + \alpha t^2}\, dt = \log(1 + \alpha t^2),$$

so that the amount accumulated after 12 years is

$$260 = 100e^{r(t)} = 100(1 + \alpha t^2).$$

We solve for $\alpha = 0.\overline{1}$. A deposit of 50 was made at after 15 years, the total amount in the account after 15 years is

$$A(15) = 100a(15) + 50.$$

We find the total accumulated in 20 years by simplifying

$$(100a(15) + 50) \left[\exp \left(\int_{15}^{20} \delta(t)\, dt \right) \right].$$

The numerical solution is 622.22.

A. 448 B. 452 C. 467 **D. 622** E. 772

6° Use the level payment duration formula to compute the duration of the annuity, bearing in mind that the formula will give us a duration measured in months. To use the formula, we must first convert the effective interest rate into a monthly effective interest rate $j = \sqrt[12]{1.075} - 1 = 0.0060$. So we calculate

$$D_{a_{\overline{n}|}} = \frac{\frac{1}{12}v + \frac{2}{12}v^2 + \cdots}{a_{\overline{n}|}}.$$

Notice that we are weighing the cash flows by fractions of the year. We simplify and compute:

$$= \frac{1}{12} \frac{(Ia)_{\overline{n}|}}{a_{\overline{n}|}}$$
$$= \frac{1}{12} \frac{\ddot{a}_{\overline{n}|} - nv^n}{1 - v^n}$$
$$= 4.44$$

In the course of computing $D_{a_{\overline{n}|}}$, we computed the present value of the annuity, $100 a_{\overline{n}|} = 8516$, which we circled in our work.

We use the bond duration formula in the same way. Calculate the per-period effective interest rate $j = {}^2\sqrt{1.075} - 1 = 0.3682$. Then

$$D_B = \frac{1}{2} \frac{Fr(Ia)_{\overline{n}|} + 1000nv^n}{Fra_{\overline{n}|} + 1000v^n}$$
$$= 12.914$$

In the course of computing D_B, we calculated the bond price as 835.89, and circled it on our page. Since we have 3 of the bonds, the total bond value is 2507.68 and the total portfolio value is 11024. The bonds represent a fraction 0.227 of the value of the portfolio. The annuity represents the rest, 0.773. The portfolio's duration is the weighted average of the durations, weighted by their value, so that $D_P = 4.44 \times 0.773 + 12.914 \times 0.227 = 6.36$.

A. 4.44 B. 6.11 **C. 6.36** D. 12.9 E. 14.8

7° If Luther was paying the fair price in 6 months, he would pay $0.5r^7(Ga)_{\overline{\infty}|i}$, where i is the effective monthly rate. However, he is expected to pay in three months, so that we must discount the price by three months. We find i by solving for it in $1 + i = \sqrt[12]{1.07}$, so that $i = 0.565\%$. The equation of value is

$$V = 0.5r^7 v^4 \frac{1}{1 - rv} = 158.61.$$

This is a price per share, so we find that the total price is 15861.

A. 8542 B. 10809 C. 13352 D. 15743 **E. 15861**

8° First, use put-call parity to solve for the risk free force of interest $r = 0.063$. Then convert r to an effective monthly interest rate $i = 0.00526$. Finally, use the duration formula for bonds, keeping in mind that we are weighting the cash-flows by fractions of a year:

$$D = \frac{20 \cdot \frac{1}{12}(Ia)_{\overline{12}|} + \frac{12}{12}1000v^{12}}{20a_{\overline{12}|} + 1000v^{12}} = 0.912$$

A. 0.78 B. 0.82 C. 0.88 **D. 0.91** E. 1.16

9° We price the bond, discounting by the spot rates.

$$P = \frac{85}{1.067} + \frac{85}{1.063^2} + \frac{85}{1.06^3} + \frac{85}{1.059^4} + \frac{1085}{1.0585^5}$$
$$= 1110.37$$

194

With this price, we find the yield rate for the bond. We recommend using the BAII Plus time value functions for this purpose. We find that $i = 5.89\%$. With the effective yield rate, we are able to find the balance after the second coupon

$$B_2 = B_0 \cdot \kappa^2 - (Fr)s_{\overline{2}|i} = 1070.02,$$

so that the interest paid in the third coupon is

$$I_3 = iB_2 = 63.02.$$

Then, the principal paid in the third coupon is $(Fr) - I_3 = 21.98$.

A. 12 B. 37 C. 52 **D. 63** E. 67

10° We like to draw cash flow diagrams for problems like these, especially for the times near the transitions between one kind of annuity and another. We must convert the nominal rate convertible quarterly into an effective monthly rate. We solve for i in

$$(1+i)^{12} = \left(1 + \frac{i^{(4)}}{4}\right),$$

so that $i = 0.00539$. We write the equation of value

$$V = 100(G\ddot{a})^{6\%}_{\overline{48}|i} + 100r^{47}v^{48}\ddot{a}_{\overline{120}|i} + 100r^{47}v^{168}(G\ddot{a})^{-2\%}_{\overline{\infty}|i}.$$

We expand this to

$$100\frac{1-(rv)^{48}}{1-rv} + 100r^{47}v^{48}\frac{1-v^{120}}{i} + 100r^{47}v^{168}\frac{1}{1-\rho v},$$

and simplify to find that $V = 173197.49$. The quantity we seek is $\kappa^{180}V = 455590.94$.

A. 173197 B. 190255 C. 398654 **D. 455591** E. 799725

11° We find cashflow diagrams useful for this kind of problem. In any case, let $r = 1.06$, so that Irene's k^{th} payment is for $100r^{k-1}$, for $k \le 10$. Her payments are constant at $100r^9$, starting with the 10th payment. Irene sells her annuity after the 8th payment. The sale price is the present value of the remaining payments at the time of the sale. We write the equation of value

$$V = 100\left[vr^8 + vr^9 a_{\overline{21}}\right] = 2025.38$$

Irene purchases $Pa_{\overline{30}}$ for 2025.38. We see that

$$P = \frac{2025.38}{a_{\overline{30}}} = 147.14.$$

A. 134.47 B. 139.48 C. 143.74 **D. 147.14** E. 153.11

12° In general, for an n period bond whose redemption value is the same as its face value, the amount of interest paid in the

k^{th} period is $F(r-i)(1-v^{n-k+1})$. For the jth bond Karen buys, its payment in the 4th period is its $(5-j)^{th}$ payment. Karen will have bought 4 bonds by the fourth period, so that the interest paid is

$$F(r-i)\left((1-v^5)+(1-v^4)+(1-v^3)+(1-v^2)\right)$$
$$= F(r-i)(4-v^5-v^4-v^3-v^2) = 18.664$$

We prefer to draw the diagram

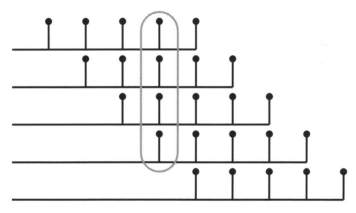

to find the relevant periods, which we circled.

A. 18.66 B. 61.34 C. 93.32 D. 306.68 E. 344.74

13° Our first step will be to find the amount of money his savings account has accumulated at the end of 15 years. No money is deposited in the first year, and for the next 9 years, 3000 is deposited every year. For the next 5 years, 7000 is deposited every year.

His deposits form an annuity $v\left(3000a_{\overline{9}|}+8000v^9a_{\overline{5}|}\right)$. The accumulated value for this annuity is

$$\kappa^{15}v\left(3000a_{\overline{9}|}+8000v^9a_{\overline{5}|}\right)=3000\kappa^5s_{\overline{9}|}+7000s_{\overline{5}|}.$$

The balance in his savings account is 77804.65. If he makes 8 level withdrawals from his savings account, the equation of value is

$$77804.65=Pa_{\overline{15}|3\%},$$

so that $P=6517.43$. If Waldo buys a 15 year annuity earning 7%, the equation of value is

$$77804.65=P'a_{\overline{15}|7\%},$$

so that $P'=8542.46$, and the difference between them is $P'-P=2025$.

A. 398 B. 720 C. 1123 D. 1756 **E. 2025**

14° First, use put-call parity to solve for $\mathcal{P}_0(65,T)=0.428466$. Recall that a box spread with exercise prices 65 and 85 is

$$(\mathcal{P}(65,T)-\mathcal{C}(65,T))-(\mathcal{P}(85,T)-\mathcal{C}(85,T)).$$

This position is a synthetic forward contract to buy for 65 and synthetic forward contract to sell for 85. This position is effectively a synthetic zero coupon bond for 20, and so the total cost is $20e^{-rT}$. So we solve for $C(85, T)$ in the system of equations

$$20e^{-rT} = P(65, T) - C(65, T) - P(85, T) + C(85, T)$$
$$10.52119 = P(85, T) + C(85, T)$$

by adding the equations and substituting for known values. We find that $C(85, T) = 1.83962$.

The butterfly spread is constructed as

$$C(65, T) - 2C(75, T) + C(85, T),$$

and its total cost is 3.42027. We solve for $C(75, T) = 5.853$.

Finally, we recognize that $P(75, T) - P(85, T)$ is a bull spread, so we use a short cut and compute the profit for $C(75, T) - C(85, T)$, an equivalent bull spread. The profit is

$$S_T - K' - (P(75, T) - P(85, T))e^{rT} = 0.92567.$$

A. 0.926 B. 1.948 C. 3.402 D. 5.855 E. 6.185

15° The loan balance at the end of the third year is

$$22460.37 = B_0 \cdot \kappa^3 - (Fr)s_{\overline{3}|i}$$

We can solve for $(Fr) = 5000$ directly, or by using the BAII Plus time value functions. With this information, we can solve for the number of loan payments. We recommend using the BAII Plus time value functions for this purpose.

There are 9 loan payments. We can calculate the value of the bond immediately after the 9th coupon directly as

$$(Fr)a_{\overline{21}|j} + Fv_j^{21} = 106,702.36,$$

or use the BAII Plus time value functions.

A. 96832 B. 102576 **C. 106702** D. 109441 E. 110440

16° First, note that the coupon payments are $Fr = 75$ per year, so that if the bond gets called in the nth year after purchase, the accumulated value is

$$75s_{\overline{n}|13.5\%} + 1000 = 2983.53.$$

We can use the BAII Plus time value functions to solve for $n = 12$.

Since the bond was priced to yield 5.4% if held to maturity, we can find the price using the basic bond formula

$$(Fr)a_{\overline{25}|i} + Fv^{25},$$

or using the BAII Plus time value functions. We note that Henrietta bought the bond immediately after the *fifth* coupon, so that there are 25 coupons left. Her price was 1284.46. However, the bond was called after 12 years. We use the BAII Plus time value function to find that her true yield for the bond is 4.4%.

A. 3.0% **B. 4.4%** C. 6.3% D. 6.4% E. 10.6%

17° Notice that Simon starts his payments and withdrawals *on* his birthday, not a month after his birthday. With that in mind, we write the equation of value

$$P\ddot{s}_{\overline{420}|j} = 8000\ddot{a}_{\overline{25}|i},$$

where j is the effective monthly rate. We find j using the equation $(1+j)^{12} = 1+i$, so that $j = 0.00526$. The other quantities are straight-forward to compute, using the standard formulas. Solving for P, we find $P = 67.47$.

A. 63.69 **B. 67.47** C. 70.05 D. 76.85 E. 85.25

18° We must compare the amount of principal with the amount Denise actually received. To that end, we use the BAII Plus time value functions to calculate the principal as $150,000$. Now, we see that her loan charged an effective yearly interest rate of 6.5%. This means that her effective monthly rate was i in $(1+i)^{12} = 1.065$, so that $i = 0.00526$. She received an amount

$$1109.53\,a_{\overline{180}|i} = 128894.4.$$

We find the point fee by solving for d in

$$150000(1-d) = 128894.4,$$

so that $d = 14.1$ points.

A. 9.75 B. 10.5 C. 12.0 **D. 14.1** E. 16.7

19° We begin by finding the price for the bond. We use the basic bond price formula

$$V = Fra_{\overline{5}|8\%} + Fv^5 = 17604.37.$$

Each coupon payment is for 1000. He makes 5 deposits into the account earning 10% interest. However, he withdraws the interest earned. In particular, the account accumulates 5000. The interest earned is redeposited into a third account. The first deposit is for 100, the next is for 200, and so on. The account accumulates at 12% interest, so we see that it accumulates $(Is)_{\overline{4}|12\%} = 1127.37$. Franz's total accumulation is 26127.37. We solve for the yield in

$$17604.37(1+i)^5 = 26127.37,$$

so that $i = 8.2\%$.

A. 7.5%   B. 7.9%   C. 8.2%   D. 8.8%   E. 9.7%

20° We can calculate Johan's interest rate by solving for i in

$$(1+i)^{24} = 7(1+i)^8,$$

so that $i = 12.9\%$. We are told that the amount in Nina's account after 9 years is the same as the amount in Johan's, so that

$$10s_{\overline{108}|j} = 500(1+i)^9 = 1493.96$$

We use the BAII Plus time value functions to find $j = 0.58\%$. After 20 years, Nina will have

$$10s_{\overline{240}|j} = 5169.48.$$

A. 2754 **B.** 5169 C. 5693 D. 6008 E. 6567

21° We write the equation of value

$$P = x_1 P_1 + x_2 P_2,$$

where x_1 is the number of 6 month bonds needed and x_2 is the number of one year bonds needed. We can find $x_2 = \frac{3000}{1040} = 2.88$. Similarly, we find that

$$x_1 = \frac{1000 - 40x_2}{1000} = 0.884$$

We can calculate the price of the 6 month bond by discounting, as

$$P_1 = \frac{1000}{1.03} = 970.87,$$

so that

$$P_2 = 1014.30 = Fr a_{\overline{2}|i} + Fv^2.$$

We use the BAII Plus time value functions to solve for $i = 3.25\%$, so that $i^{(2)} = 6.5\%$.

A. 4.2% B. 4.7% C. 6.3% **D. 6.5%** E. 6.3%

22° We begin by calculating the interest rates these perpetuities earn. Laverne's perpetuity cost 360000 and pays 10000 per year. Using the present value formula, we see that

$$360000 = 10000a_{\overline{\infty}|} = \frac{10000}{i},$$

so that $i = 0.02778$. We express the present value of Wilma's perpetuities as

$$800,000 = P \left[\frac{1}{i} + \frac{2}{j} + \frac{4}{k} \right],$$

where $j = (1+i)^2 - 1$ and $k = (1+i)^4 - 1$. We simplify the expression

$$800000 = P(36 + 35.506 + 34.53),$$

so that $P = 7544$.

A. 7544 B. 9384 C. 11423 D. 13677 E. 14346

23° Let r be the effective coupon rate per semi-annual period. We see that

$$F r a_{\overline{20}|} + C v^{20} = 1.1F \left(r a_{\overline{20}|} + v^{20} \right),$$

where $i = 3.5\%$ is the effective interest rate per period. Solving for r and substituting numerical values, we find

$$r = \frac{125 v^{20}}{100 a_{\overline{20}|}} = 0.0442.$$

The book value after the 4th coupon payment is the present value of the remaining payments then.

$$B_4 = F r a_{\overline{16}|} + C v^{16} = 1255.46,$$

and the interest paid in the 5th coupon is $I_5 = iB_4 = 43.94$.

A. 3.89 B. 9.39 C. 26.73 D. 37.43 **E. 43.94**

24° We begin by calculating her level monthly payment. We can solve for P in

$$500000 = P a_{\overline{360}|i},$$

where $i = \frac{7.3\%}{12}$, or use the BAII Plus time value functions. The level monthly payment is 3427.85. We see she would make 360 payments, so that her total payment would be 1234027.67, and the total interest paid would be 734027.67.

Now we will find the interest paid during her modified payment schedule. We begin by finding her balance after 15 years worth of monthly payments of 5000. We can use the formula

$$B_{180} = B_0(1+i)^{180} - 5000 s_{\overline{180}|i},$$

or use the BAII Plus time value functions to find that $B_{180} = 137166.59$. She has another 180 payments to make at the same interest rate, so her level payments are 1256.01. Her total payments are 1126082, so that her total interest paid is 626082. The difference between these is 107946.

A. 32000 B. 55000 C. 77000 **D. 108000** E. 184000

25° Globex did not make an interest payment in the first year. This means that the loan balance increases to $(1+i)B_0 = 1,080,000$. The subsequent interest payments are each

86400, and there are 9 of them, for a total of 777600 paid in interest over the life of the loan.

Globex did not make deposits into the fund for the first two years, but did in each subsequent year. The equation of value is

$$1,080,000 = Ds_{\overline{8}|11\%},$$

so that D = 91066.74. There were 8 deposits, so a total of 728533.91 was deposited over the life of the loan. The total payments made to service the loan were $1,506,134$.

A. 1429000 **B. 1506000** C. 1728000 D. 1882000 E. 2931000

26° We begin by solving for the interest rate i. The equation of value is

$$4444.44 = \frac{100}{i} + \frac{1}{i^2}.$$

This is a quadratic equation in $\frac{1}{i}$. Using the quadratic formula, we find that $\frac{1}{i} = 33.33$, so that i = 0.03 We find a diagram useful for setting up this problem. Eric's payments are gray.

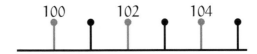

Eric's payments are two periods apart. If we define a period in terms of two of these periods, we see that the sequence of Eric's payments is an arithmetic perpetuity, fast-forwarded by a 'short' period. Define $j = (1 + i)^2 - 1 = 0.0609$. The equation of value is

$$V = (1 + i) \left(\frac{100}{j} + \frac{2}{j^2} \right) = 2246.73$$

A. 1401 B. 1479 C. 2181 **D. 2247** E. 2484

27° This is a straight-forward calculator problem. Use the BAII Plus time value functions to solve it. The only insight required is that the principal for the new loan is the balance after the 100th payment of the old loan. Use the calculator to solve for the principal on the new loan, and set that to be the future value of the old loan.

A. 7107 B. 7537 C. 8026 D. 14080 **E. 15551**

28° By transferring ownership in a year, InvesTrust forgoes two coupon payments. At current interest rates, the price of the bond in a year is the value of the remaining coupon and redemption payments. We use the BAII Plus time value function to calculate the bond price as 1085.37, being careful to convert the nominal interest rates to effective semiannual rates. We calculate the prepaid price by discounting the bond price for 2 semi-annual periods. We find that the prepaid bond price is 1036.52, so that the cost of 500 of them is 518260.

A. 518260 B. 543435 C. 547212 D. 543794 E. 578240

29° We take the derivative of the price function

$$P'(i) = -\frac{100}{i^2} - \frac{2}{i^3},$$

and write the modified duration as

$$DM = -\frac{P'(i)}{P(i)} = \frac{100 + \frac{2}{i}}{i\left(100 + \frac{1}{i}\right)}.$$

Recall that $DM = vD$, so that

$$D = (1+i)\frac{100 + \frac{2}{i}}{i\left(100 + \frac{1}{i}\right)} = 20.2$$

A. 20.2 B. 24.2 C. 27.1 D. 38.6 E. 44.1

30° Use the BAII Plus time value functions to solve this problem. Note that the question asks for the number of years.

A. 5 **B.** 6 C. 7 D. 10 E. 12

31° We begin by calculating the duration for the entire portfolio. We do this by calculating the value-weighted average of the durations.

$$\frac{1}{8}\big[(0.5 \times 4.7598) + (1.5 \times 12.3859)$$

$$+ (2.5 \times 25.987) + (3.5 \times 31.3719)\big] = 24.466$$

We are told the interest rate is 6.5%, so we calculate the modified duration for the portfolio $DM = vD = 22.97$. Finally, we use the duration price approximation

$$\Delta P \approx -DM \cdot P(i) \cdot (\Delta i) = -459455.$$

A. -460000 **B.** -451000 C. -187000 D. 53000 E. 373000

32° We begin by pricing the 30 year bond. We use the premium-discount formula, after converting the nominal coupon rate $r^{(4)}$ into an effective quarterly coupon rate $r = 2\%$ and $i^{(4)} = 5\%$ into an effective quarterly yield $i = 0.0125$. We find that the price is

$$F(r-i)a_{\overline{120}|i} + F = 1464.87.$$

The problem states that this is 15.4% more than the price of a similar bond with unknown term:

$$\frac{1464.87}{1.154} = 1269.385 = F(r-i)a_{\overline{4n}|} + F.$$

We use the BAII Plus time value functions to solve for $4n = 47.98$, so that $n = 12$ years.

Indeed, this problem can be done purely with the BAII Plus time value functions, very easily. We find the price of the 30 year bond, divide it by 1.154, set that as the price, and solve for $4n$.

A. 5 B. 7.5 **C. 12** D. 15 E. 18

33° We find I, the quarterly interest payment, by multiplying 500000 by $\frac{i^{(4)}}{4}$, so that I $= 14250$. We find D by solving for it in

$$500000 = Ds_{\overline{80}|3\%},$$

so that D $= 1555.873$. We find that TAN has been making total quarterly payments of 15805.873.

   After refinancing, TAN continues to pay the loan interest each quarter. The new quarterly interest payments are 6250. TAN continues to make the same total quarterly payment, so TAN deposits D$' = 9555.873$ each quarter. We can now write value at the end of 20 years as

$$1555.873\kappa^{68}s_{\overline{12}|3\%} + 9555.873s_{\overline{68}|3\%} - 500000,$$

a total of 1723548.45.

   A. 150000 B. 164000 C. 582000 D. 1360000 **E. 1720000**

34° We write the equation of value

$$100s_{\overline{300}|1\%} + 300s_{\overline{300}|0.6667\%} = X(Ga)_{\overline{360}|0.25\%}$$

and solve for X $= 1817.66$, recalling that

$$(Ga)_{\overline{m}|} = v\frac{1-(rv)^n}{1-rv},$$

where r $= 1.01$ and v $= \frac{1}{1.0025}$.

   A. 1117 B. 1227 **C. 1818** D. 1822 E. 2008

35° We use the geometric annuity duration formula

$$D = \frac{n(rv)^n}{1-(rv)^n} + \frac{1+i}{1+i-r} = 8.82.$$

We note that solving this problem would be time consuming and error prone without the formula.

A. 5.41 **B. 8.82** C. 27.17 D. 33.76 E. 55.89

CALCULATORS

1 TIME VALUE

In our solutions, we have frequently said "use the BAII Plus time value functions to calculate..." The BAII Plus time value functions are easy to use, though perhaps a little tricky to explain.

The basic idea is that the calculator has buttons that represent variables in loan problems:

N the number of periods;

I/Y the effective interest rate;

PV the present value;

PMT the payment;

FV the future value;

That said, we must make a brief aside to fix the calculator's settings. Press 2nd P/Y. If you have never changed this setting before, it should respond with P/Y 12.00. The calculator comes set up to assume that there are 12 periods in a year. We don't like that. Our calculations are all based around periods of varying lengths, not months. The P/Y function lets us change the number of periods, but we like to set it to 1. To do so, press 1 `ENTER` `CE/C`.

In order to set the number of periods to, say, $n = 10$, we press 10 `N` into the calculator. The calculator will respond with `N` `=` `10.00`. The other buttons operate in the same way. If you want to set a value, you type the number and press the corresponding button.

The time functions allow us to solve level payment problems involving the time values. This includes level payment annuities, bonds, and loans. In order to solve for a variable, we enter data for all of the other variables, and hit `CPT` `VAR`, where `VAR` is the variable we want to find. When we are done solving a problem, we must press 2nd `CLR` `TVM` to clear the time value variables. We do not want variables from the last problem getting mixed up with variables from the new problem. Think of it as calculator hygiene.

Let us do an example. Press

`12 N 2.5 I/Y 1000 FV CPT PMT.`

The calculator will respond with `PMT=` `-72.49`. We calculated the monthly level payment for a 1000 dollar 12 period loan at an effective interest rate of 2.5%. Notice that the `PMT` value is negative. The calculator adopts the convention that positive values are receivable, and negative amounts are payable. You might have noticed that we did not set the `PV` variable. That's okay, the calculator will assume that the present value is 0. This shortcut is one of the reasons why calculator hygiene is important. If the last problem we worked on had a PV value set, we would have gotten a nonsense answer. Enter 2nd CLR TVM.

Let's do another example. This time, you want to find the present value of a bond that pays 30 each period for 5 years, has a redemption value of 1000, and yields $i^{(2)} = 7\%$. Try it yourself before reading on. We enter

> 10 N 3.5 I/Y 30 PMT 1000 FV CPT PV

and the calculator responds with PV = -958.42. Now, let's find out what the yield would be if we changed the number of years to, say, 10, so that $N = 20$. We enter 20 N CPT I/Y, and the calculator responds with I/Y= 3.29. This feature is useful for dealing with callable bonds, for example.

Let's do a harder one. Suppose that a bank account earns interest at an effective rate of 5%. Suppose that after 5 periods, interest rates shift to 6%. You make a deposit of 100 at the end of each period. How much will you have accumulated in 10 periods?

We enter

> 5 N 5 I/Y 100 - PMT CPT FV - PV 6 I/Y CPT FV

The first part of this calculation should be straight-forward to understand. In typing 5 N 5 I/Y 100 - PMT CPT FV, we calculated the accumulated value in the first five years. And the answer was FV = 552.56. By entering - PV, we set the accumulated value to be the present value – we effectively fast-forwarded the account to the 5th period. Now, when we calculate the accumulated value for the next 5 years, at 6%, we will be calculating the accumulated value for the entire 10 years the account was active. We see that the answer is 1303.16.

One further important variation. We have been discussing situations where payments are made at the end of the month. How do we calculate time values when payments are made at the beginning? We can use the same calculator techniques, but we must change another setting.

Suppose that a bank account earns interest at an effective rate of 5%. Suppose that after 5 periods, interest rates shift to 6%. You make a deposit of 100 at the *beginning* of each period. How much will you have accumulated in 10 periods? Press

```
2nd BGN 2nd SET CE/C 5 N 5 I/Y 100 - PMT CPT FV -
                  PV 6 I/Y CPT FV
```

We see the answer is 1373.96. It is **vital**[1] to change the BGN setting back to END. It is not reset by clearing the time value variables, and the answers the calculator produces look plausible. Indeed, they are only off by one period's worth of interest. Do *not* make this mistake. It can easily ruin your day.

2 CASHFLOWS, IRR, AND NPV

The BAII Plus also has facilities for calculating the internal rate of return for non-level cash flows. To use the facility,

---

1 This is the only time we have used a boldfaced font in the *entire book*.

we must enter the cash flows. Press CF, and the calculator will respond with CFo= 0.00. Press 100 - ENTER and the calculator will respond with CFo= -100.00. We can think of the CFo variable as representing the amount paid to enter the investment at time 0. Now, press ↓, the down-arrow, and the calculator will respond with C01 0.00. This is the first cash flow. Let's set it to 55, by pressing 55 ENTER ↓. The calculator responds with F01 1.00. We can set the number of times that we get paid C01 by changing the F01 value. We get paid once by default, so press ↓ again, and then press 50 ENTER ↓↓ 45 ENTER. We have keyed in the sequence of cash flows $\{-100, 55, 50, 45\}$. We can find its internal rate of return by pressing IRR CPT.

We can also calculate the net present value for the sequence. Press NPV. The calculator will respond with I= 0.00. We set the prevailing interest rate at 5% and calculate the net present value by pressing 5 ENTER ↓ CPT. The calculator responds with NPV= 36.61.

INDEX

accumulation function, 17
American option, 128
amortization
    bond premiums, 77
    interest principal, 70
    loan principal, 70
amortization of bond premiums, 77
amount function, 18
annual percentage rate, 69
annuity
    arithmetic, 59
    decreasing, 57
    deferred, 54
    due, 52
    geometric, 60
    immediate, 52
    increasing, 55
    scaled, 54
    unit, 53
APR, 69
arbitrage, 5
arithmetic

    perpetuity, 62
arithmetic annuity, 59
arithmetic perpetuity, 62
ask price, 1
at-the-money, 132

back-to-back loan, 120
basic pricing principle, 22
bear spread, 138
Bermudan option, 128
bid-ask spread, 1
bond, 74
    amortization of premiums, 77
    callable, 78
    coupon, 75
    coupon rate, 75
    discount, 76
    face value, 75
    par value, 75
    premium, 76
    premium-discount formula, 76

Made in the USA
Charleston, SC
09 May 2016